DECLARE DISUNION
The Struggle to Save Liberty in America

J. PETERSON

CONTENTS

1   Overview   1

2   The Common Man   4

3   The Indictment   10

4   The Federal Complex Considered   17

5   Splinter Groups   35

6   Money and No Money   64

7   Money and Power   77

8   Managed Economies   100

9   The Free Market   139

10 Professional and Private Armies   149

11 Borders   155

12 Growing the Federal Complex   161

13 The Action Plan   149

OVERVIEW

A book of this nature and title should have an overview so that you know the general directions in which the author is heading. To begin with, I wrote this book because no matter for whom Americans vote, the government heads only in one direction: towards more control over our lives and a loss of liberty. How can we continue to be a free people when our assets are seized to pay off the losses of investment companies, the government develops private armies, and on and on?

The premise herein is that the federal legislators and elected federal officials are part of a larger complex, the "federal complex", composed of legislators, elected officials, lobbyists, foundations, think-tanks, commissions, law firms, boards, and other institutions in Washington, all of whom feed one another morally and financially, and expand the control of the federal government through legislation and regulation. As government control expands, our liberty shrinks. This federal complex believes that it knows what is best for America. The greatest nation that has ever drawn a breath now has a government that is sitting on and crushing down its only real asset, the "common man", the men and women who built this nation.

In the 1780's when our Constitution was written, this federal complex did not exist. The federal government was a few hundred legislators, elected executive officials, and appointees trying to keep a nation together. They did not foresee that this complex would evolve nor could they have imagined its momentum. Consequently, there is no constitutional counterbalance to the power and momentum of the complex.

How then do we stop this federal complex, this Washington establishment, from legislating the death of our liberty? What can possibly balance the power of Washington? The answer is the states. They were the answer in 1776 and they are the answer now. We must encourage our individual state governments to take action to protect our liberty, our God-given right to the Promise and Hope of America. There are no other entities in America that have the power to balance the complex. The states rebelled against England, their lawful sovereign, because they had the obligation to defend liberty and the courage to undertake that defense. They still have that obligation. The states, individually and severally, must instruct the federal complex, on threat of disunion, to cease its encroachments on the liberty of its citizens.

The last chapter encompasses specific action that the states should take to correct the imbalance. We Americans are and should be one people, despite the predations of the federal complex to isolate and separate us into hyphenated voting blocs. Disunion is not the "s" word; it is not secession. Disunion is pulling away to establish a new framework for governing all Americans, a framework in which the individual states insist that the federal government honor the principles set forth in the Declaration of Independence.

God bless us all.

"When in the Course of human Events, it becomes necessary for one People to dissolve the Political Bands which have connected them with another ...... "

The Declaration of Independence, 1776

CHAPTER ONE

The Common Man

America's success belongs to the common man. America has allowed that man to work his wonders. And these wonders are so plain, so simple, so by-God common and everyday that we hardly ever see them for the wonders they are. It is the wonder of a guy in Nebraska who gets up every morning and goes to an everyday job to put food on his table and dreams that his kids will have it better. It is the wonder of a woman in Maryland whose husband has been hurt who thinks that she can sell her quilts on the internet to keep a roof over her family's heads, it is the high school kid in Oregon whose parents can't speak English who stays up late to study for a science test, and the old couple in the Bronx who set up a shelter for the homeless in an abandoned church. The idea that is America has imbued those men and women with the hope to dream dreams of unparalleled prosperity, security, and liberty. They're little dreams, every one of them, but put them together, knead them into a bread, and they're so big they rise over the edges like the head of a warm loaf. America says, "Come, join us. Be truly free to live and dream." America is a beacon of hope in the world. America says to the humblest beggar, to the least of us, "Come, and I'll give you an even roll to make or break your dream."

What a nation! What a gift of God to all men everywhere!

We are in danger of losing that America, and losing means not just slipping from our place as the strongest economy to that of a second or third stringer, but also to a loss of freedom: a diminution of our God-given rights to life, liberty, and the pursuit of happiness. We are in danger not from the Republicans or the Democrats, but because we have permitted the growth of a federal complex in Washington that now proceeds along its own course no matter who is voted in or out. We find staggering deficits that will hostage our grandchildren's livelihoods, enormous amounts of money pledged to protect private commercial losses, and a seeming cession of our southern borders to illegal incursions. These things happen because the goals of this federal complex are not the goals of the citizenry. It simply does not matter for whom we vote.

The growing threat to us now is that this federal complex has tools- such as maintaining and strengthening voting blocs based on ethnic or religious groups- that will enhance and accelerate the power of this complex. It is no longer realistic to expect that we can affect the growth or direction of the federal complex through the representatives whom we send to Washington. The only way that Americans can still hope to retain their historic freedoms is to step back from working for change to the unchangeables in Washington, and instead insist that the individual state governments step forward and protect them. The state governments are the only political entities in this nation that still have the leverage and power to protect the liberty and rights of their citizens. And more than that, they have the obligation to do so. It was these same states, after all, that created this federal government which birthed the complex. Now it is time for you to insist that your state defend you from the power of this federal complex, this Washington establishment.

This book is to encourage you as you undertake this arduous and perilous task.

The Promise and the Hope

The promise of America is not the promise of success; it is the promise that you get a fair shot at achieving that success, that you get the same odds as the next man or woman. The hope of everyone is that they will succeed and that their children will have a better or easier life. The Promise and the Hope, that is America in a nutshell.

America has always been the land of dreamers and doers. The nation has been so successful, and by that I mean that it has offered such a high standard of living to so many, because of both these dreamers and doers. The Promise of America is that you get a fair shot, the same shot as your neighbor, and the Hope is that you will be let alone to bring your dream to a reality, whether that dream is a decent job, a bigger house, your own business, or college for your kids. The Promise is that it does not matter how poor you are, or who your parents are, or where you went to school or where you go or don't go to church. You work hard, roll the bones, and improve the odds for your children. A lot of times it doesn't work. It's bad timing, bad work, or bad luck. But then you get up and get another a shot because America really does not care if you flubbed it the first time, or the first fifty times.

Sometimes you roll the bones, and it kills you. When the first colonists came to these shores they had mortality rates of thirty, fifty, or eighty percent. They buried wives, husbands, children, and even whole families. Sometimes the entire colony died or just disappeared, like Roanoke. Even as late as the 1840's the German immigrants in south Texas lost over half their numbers. But they stuck it out because they saw a glimpse, a hope, that their life could be better, that maybe their children would prosper. Immigrants wrested a life from the wilderness and from disease, hunger, loneliness, death, savages, drought, and anyone and anything else. Their children, if they survived, had it better. And they did it themselves. They enjoyed the liberty to succeed and the liberty to fail. Government, if there was any, was local. They formed local governments for their schools, for safety, and to promote their efforts together.

Federal and state governments have tried to enhance both the Promise and the Hope. They tried to assure everyone of an even chance with laws which prohibit discrimination and which enhance access to opportunities for everyone. And these governments also tried to enhance the chances by providing free education and numerous other programs that encourage commercial enterprises.

The Promise and the Hope took the common man, men and women who came here from next door and from Timbuktu, gave him the liberty to succeed or to fail, and turned him loose. The world has never been the same.

"... a History of repeated Injuries and Usurpations, all having in direct Object the Establishment of an absolute Tyranny over these States."

The Declaration of Independence, 1776

CHAPTER TWO

The Indictment

Now we are losing that America, that great dream, that liberty that makes America what it is. We are losing the Promise and the Hope. It is not the common man who is in danger of failing, but the government complex that has betrayed that man, and will consume his liberty and his future, and his children's future. How can this be when the purposes of the federal government were set forth so clearly: "...to form a more perfect Union, establish Justice, insure domestic Tranquility, provide for the common defence, promote the general Welfare, and secure the blessings of Liberty..."?

But let the condemnation not rest on generalities. This federal government complex has:

1. declined to protect its citizenry from intrusions by foreign entities, groups, and individuals;

2. created splinter groups, multi-generational sub-classes of government-dependent families and individuals;

3. created private armies to which it has ceded military and police powers to engage in reckless foreign wars financed by future generations, and which can be used to enforce its policies in our homeland;

4. created entities to which it has ceded its commercial and financial powers, and which are not accountable to the people;

5. pledged the resources of private citizens to guarantee the viability and underwrite the losses of preferred commercial enterprises;

6. seized the resources of private citizens through its taxing power and transferred those resources to preferred commercial enterprises;

7. pledged the future resources of private citizens to guarantee the viability of preferred commercial enterprises.

These charges are an indictment of the federal government complex. These charges go to the foundation of our governance and the liberty we enjoy as Americans and as human beings. The Declaration of Independence acknowledged our right to life, liberty, and the pursuit of happiness as coming from God. No government may contravene those rights without suffering consequences.

The issue is whether we Americans, as a people, will accept our government's contraction of those rights. Because of the growth and power of the federal government complex, the process by which we elect our federal representatives is compromised and will become even more so. In these times when our own national government ceases to serve the people but instead seeks to become our master, the people must look to the creators of the national government for relief and protection of their liberty: the separate and individual states. It is incumbent on the states to protect the liberty of their citizenry. They did it in the 1770's and can do so again. This is not a matter of state rights. It is a matter of human rights and the obligation of each state to defend them from the encroachments of the federal complex, even if it means redefining the union.

The federal government complex stands indicted. Few people who value their freedom and their liberty would agree with any of these actions taken by the government. Certainly no private citizen voted in favor of any one of them. In the face of the overwhelming and growing power of the federal government complex, the individual citizen can seemingly do little. Nothing you or I do in the next election, the one after that, or the one following will make any substantive change. The Democrats will promise a nickel, the Republicans will claim that is irresponsible and promise a dime, but it is business as usual, and that business is expanding the governance over the nation. This federal government complex is wasting the Promise and the Hope of America.

The federal complex did not set out to do it; it was not deliberate. The complex just did not care. The Promise and Hope of America simply do not matter to a government complex that assumes that the citizenry exists for the sake of the complex. The problem for Americans now is that the Constitution does not contain the balance or the antidote for a federal government complex intent on expansion. Americans now must look outside the Constitution to the creators of the federal government and the federal government complex.

The term "federal government complex" or "federal complex" is used throughout this book. This complex is the elected federal legislators, the appointed and elected high level policymakers, lobbyists, boards, czars, consultants, political foundations, top military personnel, and law firms and others who engage directly or indirectly in the executive and legislative processes of government. I do not mean to include the general federal employees engaged in various activities such as clerks, armed forces personnel, the Corps of Engineers, NASA, NIH, CDC, or the hundred other agencies and the hundreds of thousands of people engaged in providing service. I am focusing on those individuals who are the momentum behind the increasingly threatening federal action charged in the indictment above.

How often do we hear that some candidate, or a commentator, or a political guru wants to cut the number of government employees by ten, twenty, or fifty percent? The government employees are not the problem; they have never been the problem. The problem is the complex. The problem is the tens or hundreds of thousands of Washington "insiders", the "Establishment". They are the ones who daily sap the strength of America, who feed on the Promise and the Hope. They develop, change, write, modify, analyze, propose, oppose, and pontificate upon legislation, regulation, and running the American dream into the ground. The complex is a way of doing business. It expands the control of the government into every area of our lives. The complex has grown over the past two hundred and some odd years. Its growth accelerated phenomenally after WWII, and for the past thirty years it has found ways and tools to grow still faster. The complex grows; it succeeds by controlling more and more of the life of the common man. It succeeds by twisting the Promise and the Hope into something lifeless that it can use to control still more. The complex is not vulnerable to any political process because it is the political process.

It is not some massive conspiracy out to get us. Instead, it is a push, a mighty wind. There are thousands of organizations, boards, commissions, foundations, firms, committees, companies, and bureaus, composed of hundreds of thousands of persons, each intent on succeeding and expanding their influence and control. Together they are a mighty wind moving the government further into the lives of every American through regulation and legislation. They do it because that is where there is money and power.

The Constitution does not contemplate the possibility of a powerful government complex because the Founders never considered it. The government envisioned by the Founders sought to balance powers among the judicial, legislative, and executive branches. They did not envision the complex so they did not see a need for a counterweight, or a balance to its power. The Founders were merchants, farmers, doctors, or lawyers whose livelihoods did not depend on securing elections or feeding at the public's expense. In fact, their forays into the public arena were burdens to them, taking them from their businesses and families. They truly were public servants, men who did what they did on behalf of the interests of their fellow citizens, many feeling truly obligated because they had been blessed with money or education. Look at the men and women now who call themselves public servants: persons who have not held a real job for decades, who have grown wealthy feeding off of the common man. They stay in power not because they are our efficient servants, but because they are part of and have tapped into the federal complex. The complex funds them, grooms them, nourishes them, and secures their future, both as legislators or among the ranks of the complex as lobbyists or consultants.

Is there a federal complex? Of course. Look at the Washington phonebook for the law firms, the political foundations, the lobbyists, the committees, the special interests, the boards, the think-tanks, and the commissions. But is this federal complex the murderer, the wanton killer of the Promise and the Hope of America? You think not? Then show me the Washington, the Jefferson, Madison, or Adams of our day. There are no such men or women there today. They are not wanted by the complex because when their liberty was threatened, they took up arms and rebelled. They made a revolution.

"He has combined with others to subject us to a Jurisdiction foreign to our Constitution."

The Declaration of Independence, 1776

CHAPTER THREE

The Federal Complex Considered

The federal complex is ten thousand or a hundred thousand legislators, lobbyists, aides, lawyers, economists, consultants, and brokers all working independently today or in groups tomorrow, but all with the same goal: to succeed. The complex is as minor as a lobbyist seeking a change in the tax law for depreciation, or as sinister as a lawyer for the arms industry golfing with a general and whispering into his ear that it's a good time for a war. It is a hundred conservative institutes and a hundred liberal think-tanks analyzing new legislative initiatives and preparing internet campaigns to raise money. Each of them wants to succeed, do well, grow and prosper, and when they do, the power of the government will expand. The government will move further into our lives. Those in the complex share the conceit that if only their idea prevails, all will be well; that they know what is best for the common man. So a commission tells the chief executive that unless he commits hundreds of billions of dollars to back failed banks and investment houses that the economy will collapse. Their conceit is boundless. They gave us "nation building" in the Middle East, trillion dollar deficits, and private armies that are an infestation.

The complex moves to promote dependence on government programs and offers protection to privileged voter blocs, all the while hollowing out liberty like a termite army in a log. Individuals and organizations in the complex may not agree with one another, do not all push in the same direction. In fact they are successful precisely because they do not agree. They advise alternative courses, analyze them, debate them, hire consultants, and raise gobs of money to oppose or propose. From the perspective of the common man, it makes no difference which side wins. The common man loses and the complex succeeds. The power and control of the government expands and liberty recedes.

This government complex, all of the legislators, consultants, top bureaucrats, lobbyists, large foundations, and law firms, need the government to be a successful growth industry. If the government's power stops expanding, then the law firms, the foundations, and all the rest of the complex stops growing, campaign finances dry up, and powerful people join the unemployment line. This urge for success and growth is not because the federal complex is wicked or evil, but because it is a human endeavor and it is the nature of the human animal, whether a lone hunter with a stone-tipped spear, or a multi-national corporation, or a lobbyist firm, to want to succeed. That is why it does not matter which party is in power, it does not matter what kind of reform legislation is proposed, or for whom you vote in the next election. Whatever happens, the government complex will move towards more control over the lives of Americans. The complex erodes individual liberty, discourages initiative, and increases its management of all aspects of the economy. It will kill the Promise and the Hope. And do not be so naive as to think that the complex can centrally manage the economy and we will still be a free people. That is a fallacy.

We look at the complex and see only the thousands of firms, organizations, companies, commissions, agencies, bureaus, and foundations, but not their combined affect. That affect is like a strong wind blowing a ship towards the rocks. Always, the wind is blowing. The ship may drop anchor to stop its progress, but the next captain weighs the anchor and we are blown closer. The ship never goes back, it never regains the ground lost, and the push is inexorable. That is why it does not matter whether there is a Republican or a Democrat in the White House, or a majority of one party in Congress. We are moving in the same direction no matter who is there. Sometimes we move a bit faster than others, but it is always towards the rocks. The wind only blows in one direction.

The pages ahead lay out the affects of this complex on America. More than just the affects, this book affirms that all fifty states are obligated to protect the liberty of their citizens and the dream of America from the encroachments of the federal complex. The states can do so by reordering the manner in which in which they permit the federal government to affect the citizenry, by changing or amending the Constitution. The federal complex will attempt to stop any such amendments from taking place in the prescribed form set forth for amendments to the Constitution. There is simply too much money and too much power for the complex to accept a fundamental change. The federal complex, through its expanded powers and support, will almost certainly move to stop or dilute any such action. At that point, the states must consider actions such as disunion, and seek to relate to the federal government in a non-traditional manner.

Consider the beginnings of the government in the 1780's. There simply were no laws on the books at all. The federal congress built legislation from the ground up. They were not tweaking or smoothing things out; they were building a body of legislation. Laws were passed that addressed specific needs at specific times, but with each succeeding legislative term times changed and so did the needs. But instead of calling into question the legislative initiative, additional laws were stacked on so as to make the law more or less responsive. This federal complex absorbs the law, and then nourishes lobbyists, law firms, and consultants to deal with it and to control it. The last thing the complex wants is to have the law end. The complex wants it expanded, adjusted, improved, and, of course, the all-time favorite: "reformed". We no longer question the wisdom of certain initiatives. Instead we talk about filling in loopholes, or creating them, because that is what the complex is good at and encourages.

Look at the income tax legislation. In that one initiative the federal government was enabled to rummage through and squeeze the purse of the common man. Now, entire industries have built up around the tax code. Not just the lobbyists and consultants, but tax preparers, software developers, depreciation specialists, investment companies, 1031 exchangers, and a host of others. The question of whether the federal government complex should be in our purse never is asked. The question of whether the income tax promotes "the general Welfare" no longer is given relevance. Yet it is this same tax that has funded the growth of the federal government and much of the complex. With this tax the federal complex put the taxpayer directly on the hook. Not one person alive today ever considered these questions at a time when the questions really mattered: when the income tax was being considered. Yet, here we are, and here is the income tax. We will return to this drain on the common man in later chapters.

Once in a generation comes truly monumental legislation that significantly expands the role of the government in our lives. The most recent was the healthcare legislation passed in 2010. This law is hundreds of pages and will provide grist for the complex as long as this nation lasts. We glimpsed the mindset of the complex with the immortal pronouncement of one of the bill's supporters who suggested that the legislators needed to pass the bill so that they could see what it contained. The bills, the laws, the regulations do not matter to the complex. What matters is that it expands control over the life of the common man.

If a bill contains the word "reform" in its title, the taxpayer can rest assured that his wallet is going to the cleaners. If it contains the word "patriot", then his human rights are going to take a beating. At its most benign each legislative session looks at how to fix, correct, or equalize an existing law. This is much easier than examining whether or not the law should be there at all. There is tremendous pressure from inside the federal complex to keep laws, and, more than that, to keep adjusting or "tweaking" them. The federal legislators themselves are part of and will always back the complex. It is the source of their money and their power.

The Founders could have foreseen the development of this complex. They knew that the monarchies surrounded themselves with royal courts, the government complexes of their day. These were people who seemed to stay forever, who pushed only pro-monarchical policies by their sheer weight. Perhaps the Founders saw these monarchical courts or complexes as phenomena of hereditary autocracies, and such complexes would have no place in the republic that they envisioned in the New World. But the complex is here. The federal complex has restricted individual liberty and will restrict it further. It is a fat cat devouring a mouse.

Had the Founders foreseen the growth of the federal complex, they could have created a balance to its power just as they developed what they hoped would be self-limiting powers to the three branches set out in the Constitution. But they did not balance the federal complex because they did not imagine it. So now it is our obligation to correct that oversight, to balance the federal complex before it forever swallows the Promise and the Hope. That balance can only be found in the entities that are still strong enough to defend the liberty of the citizenry: the states.

But one can sit back and say that the federal government is simply regulating a more intricate economy for our protection. It would be great if that "simply" was true. But what is happening is that as the federal government complex moves to concentrate power in itself, it also moves to concentrate wealth. Power and wealth walk hand in hand. One does not always have to precede the other, but one always accompanies the other. For example, as America grew wealthier, it became more powerful on the international scene. As China becomes wealthier, its influence becomes more powerful. So too, as the federal complex concentrates power, it concentrates wealth.

The federal complex is succeeding. It has grown, and now it is stifling the Promise and the Hope of America. Americans suspect that there is no longer an even shake to the dice because there are groups privileged by the government who, in return for supporting the growth of the government, get what appears to be a better shake. And the hope of a better life for the next generation? It has all but disappeared. A terrible discontent creeps through the nation, a surliness, a deep worry that something almost indefinable has gone wrong. We vote, usually without enthusiasm, and often "against" rather than "for". Rarely, but occasionally, a hero, someone for whom many Americans have high hopes, appears on the horizon, but it is business as usual, and business as usual means that the federal complex is moving America in the direction that the federal complex wants to go: towards more control over the lives of Americans.

Sometimes Americans respond in anger and sometimes even in violence. Most of the time the anger gives rise to political movements that blow like clouds across the political landscape for a season or two and are gone to become footnotes in the history of the country.

The violence, the political movements, are all vanities. There were the riots of the 1960's and 70's. They grabbed headlines and then disappeared. The political movements have always fared the same. Both the violence and the movements allow segments of the electorate to blow off steam, to eliminate some of their frustration in a relatively harmless way. Political movements blaze up, illuminate some tender area of the electorate for a moment, and then their ashes are shoveled aside. They make little impact, but allow the participants the illusion that they are in control and making a difference. The government complex continues to swell and gnaw at liberty. At best the gnawing stops for a few years, but there are chunks of flesh missing, and then the gnawing starts again like some old horror picture come to life and where we have been cast unwillingly in the starring roles.

These third parties expect to rise up and swing mighty blows, but they hit only air. They have trouble even identifying their target. It is "liberals", or "conservatives", or "government waste", or the "industrial complex". They only know that somewhere someone is gutting the nation. It is this federal complex that has grown, that feeds on chaos, legislation, and strife. And its affect is this wind that moves the federal government which it supports and nourishes.

There are two particular reasons why our system has accelerated the growth of the power of this complex. The first reason is political, and second is financial. The first is the nature of politics as it has grown around the Constitution to create internal pressure in the government complex to expand its control. Presidents and members of congress are known for the legislation they enact, not the legislation they do not enact or the legislation that they revoke. When legislation is enacted, someone receives a benefit. Once that happens, there is virtually never a reason to go back and undo it. In fact there is the strongest of incentives for a legislator not to undo any laws. Once the legislation is passed then the governmental complex and economic system adjust to that new law, the government bureaucracy expands to enforce it, arrangements are made, consultants are hired, and interest groups are formed. Undoing the legislation will simply arouse the ire of whoever succeeded in getting the legislation passed in the first place, and the ire of whoever is enforcing it, without any consequent benefit to the legislator. Even if the legislation was just plain bad law and its affects generally pernicious, it is over, the hurt has happened. It is a poor use of the legislator's own time and resources to place a band aid on an existing cut when he needs to be focused on creating benefits if he is to be re-elected.

If the legislation has given a benefit to someone, then that person would be irate at its loss and angry at the legislator. It is far better for the legislator to expand the happy person's benefits and even determine if more persons can be added. The natural momentum of the legislative branch is to increase legislation and regulation. And we should remember the obvious: each legislative session becomes the baseline for the one following. The question to each legislator is, "What did you do this session?".

The second special reason for the growth of the federal complex is money. There is a financial push to expand the control of the government complex. Legislators must have pending or threatened legislation to make deals with special interest groups to acquire the financial resources to mount effective campaigns. For the legislative system to churn there must be threatened legislation with government staff to analyze it, consultants to ponder it, special interests groups lobbying for and against it, the promise and reality of campaign contributions, the campaign consultants and organizers, fund raisers, and on and on. And with each new legislative initiative the government complex grows.   A session without new and controversial legislation is a session without sunshine.

The federal complex rewards the elected legislators and all who enter its fold. It provides them with money to continue what they are doing: developing, expanding, contracting, revising, proposing, critiquing, implementing, and analyzing existing, new, or proposed legislation and regulation. As long as those functions are happening, as long as the federal complex is growing, money flows into campaign coffers, and there are legal fees, foundation income, lobbyists, and political war chests. It does not matter what party is in power or for whom you vote in the next election; the federal complex grows and liberty contracts. Furthermore it even rewards the incumbent who is defeated who can then function as a consultant or a lobbyist.

So, there is the political pressure to make a benefit, and the financial pressures to create new initiatives and legislation. The federal government has grown in the same manner that other human endeavors tend to grow. This has been a natural growth, the propensity of any human endeavor to succeed and to expand. The complex gets bigger and more powerful simply because it can.   The government complex thrives on legislation, any legislation will do, but the best is that which expands control of the complex. It is both money and power to the legislators, law firms, consultants, and political foundations: the government complex.

The government complex does not have the power to change its own path, to re-direct itself, because it is not a matter of policy, but of nature. The federal complex can no more decide to stop its abrogation of liberty than could the monarchical courts. The nature of the complex is to expand and consolidate power. The complex grows each year and its control over the lives of Americans grows with it. The legislation and regulations it belabors consume or control a larger share of the GDP through borrowing, taxation, and, just as effectively, creating dependence.

Americans, perpetual optimists, think that all will be corrected in the next election if only we vote for the right candidates or change the party in power, or if only we can get a tax cut, or maybe tax just the top ten percent of incomes. Then there is the great favorite, the reform candidates who represent an angry electorate and promise to bring a "fresh perspective" to Washington. The only changes that occur are short term policy changes that may nominally cut back this or that service, until it is time for the next initiative, the next great leap forward. How many of our federal legislators support the concept of "smaller government", whatever that term means? Almost certainly the vast majority would subscribe to the proposition that government should be smaller. How many legislators have even run on that proposition as an explicit campaign promise to their constituents? Some? All? Most? For the last ten, fifty, or one hundred years? It simply makes no difference. The momentum of the federal government complex carries it forward to more control.

Size does not matter. Not so many years ago a vice president came on one television program or another and announced to the nation that in keeping with that administration's campaign promises, he had just finished shrinking the government, re-made it into something smaller, nimbler, and better. No one knew what he was talking about. Even the pundits scratched their heads. We may have too many federal employees, too few, or the number may be just right. The problem is not the number of federal employees because they are not part of the federal complex. The threat to our liberty is from the aura of powerful entities around the legislators, and the legislators themselves. This federal complex always moves to increase power for the federal government.

So, one might ask, what is different now? These pressures for the federal complex to expand have been with us for over two hundred years and will be with us forever. What is different is the breadth of the indictment. Those charges could not have been made one hundred years ago or thirty years ago. What is different now is that the complex is achieving the critical mass which will forever smother the Promise and the Hope of America. What is different now is that the federal complex has developed the tools to expand its controls over Americans more rapidly. And these tools are beginning to yield results. With these tools, which the federal complex has given itself, the growth of the complex is accelerating.

The primary tool is "splinter groups". A splinter group is any identifiable ethnic, social, cultural, or labor group that has been peeled off from the larger electorate and placed in a position by the federal complex where it is dependent on the complex for protection. That protection may be financial, political, legal, real, or just perceived as real by the splinter group. The splinter group's dependence on the federal complex means that the complex has a voting bloc that it can count on to support the growth and expansion of its power to control the common man.

In the next chapter we will look at the splinter groups. But first it is important to emphasize that the picture is not one of hopelessness, of a ship pushed inexorably to its end. In the last hundred years the power and the scope of control of the federal government has increased beyond imagining, but there are still entities that can counterbalance this power, this control. The states, singly or in combination, can do it. We will have fifty chances to affect change, to save the Promise and the Hope. All we need is a few that will make clear to the federal complex that the complex will not proceed further on this course. Such a stand by a few states or even all of them cannot destroy the federal complex, cannot turn back the clock to days when a few hundred farmers, lawyers, and merchants were the government. The federal complex is an organic, not an incidental growth. There should have been a strong constitutional counterbalance to the federal complex, but there is not because the Founders did not foresee it. A federal government, any federal government, will birth its own complex. What even a small group of states can be is the counterweight, the balance to this complex. They can say "No"; they will not permit the indicted offenses to be inflicted further on their citizens. They can deny the federal government the power to offend the God-given liberty of its citizens.

In the 1770's the thirteen colonies rebelled against their lawful national government. Those Americans rebelled because they wanted to be free of oppression by that government. They wanted to be free of its restriction. Had you asked them to tell you in a word what they were seeking, that word would be "liberty", the God given right of every human being to be let alone to pursue their life as they think best. Contrary to all expectations, the struggle succeeded. The issue was never to live without government. Even the fomenters of this rebellion had served and continued to serve in local and colonial legislatures. These rebels were the intellectual children of Voltaire, Rousseau, and a century of English philosophers. Anarchy was never the goal. They wanted a well ordered government that would promote the public welfare.

But the Founders were concerned that a national government could become oppressive, would restrict liberty, so they sought to put restraints on it. Taking a cue from Montesquieu, one of the restraints was to design a government that would have built-in balances to stop the natural momentum of the government to gather power to itself. They wanted to design a system that would form internal balances. They split the powers among three different branches: the legislative, executive, and judicial. They sought a government that would minimize the infringements on personal liberty, but would still be able to carry out its function of promoting the public welfare. But there was also another split in governmental power to protect against a natural propensity towards aggrandizement of power by this federal creature they were creating.

There were the states. In the Constitution all of the powers not expressly given to the federal government are reserved for the states. The states were not afterthoughts or the poor stepchildren. They were the repository for power not expressly given to a federal government. It was not the federal government which rebelled; it was not the federal government that gave us the Declaration of Independence. The federal government did not even exist until after the revolution. It was the colonies, the proto-states, that made a rebellion. And it was a rebellion born in action and violence. It was the states that acted, both alone and in concert through the Continental

Congress, to protect the liberty of the citizenry. It was the states that declared a rebellion in the name of liberty. And now, again in the name of liberty, they might be called upon to declare themselves in disunion with their own creature, this federal government and its complex.

"We hold these Truths to be self-evident, that all Men are created equal, that they are endowed by their Creator with certain unalienable Rights..."

The Declaration of Independence, 1776

CHAPTER FOUR

Splinter Groups and the Cabbage Patch Theory of Nationhood

Not so many years ago Cabbage Patch dolls were the rage and every child had to have one. It was a clever play on the old nursery story that children come from the cabbage garden and are found by their parents among the large spreading leaves. The federal complex views the citizenry in the same way, as though we are a people without a history, not a nation of people but three hundred million persons just arrived from the vegetable garden. It is easier for the complex to view us this way. In fact, they insist on it. If we claim a history as a nation, the complex says it is a history of shame. If we say that we share values, the complex says that we are not perfect and that makes any values hypocritical. The federal complex tells us that it makes no difference whether we owe allegiance to America, to a foreign country, to a drug lord or a terrorist mullah, we are all the same; we will pay AIG for its losses and can all expect equal humiliations at the airports. The complex assumes that it is all the same, a warm body is a warm body; an economic unit is an economic unit. But in truth the common man is so much more than an economic unit.

This country, this America arose at a specific time and place in history. It was an accident of history that the eastern seaboard, save for Florida, was claimed by England and had been settled by men and women primarily from northern Europe who were of a low enough status in life to be unencumbered by inherited wealth and titles. It was due to their endurance, strength, and faith that they and their descendants carved homes out from the wilderness and pushed back the frontier to the Appalachians. It was to their credit that they had developed the resources and ambition to become educated in the classics and were familiar with the thoughts of the leading philosophers of their time. And it was their good fortune that at the time when their dissatisfaction ripened into rebellion that England was at sword points with France. A twist of history here or there and America would have been stillborn or never conceived at all.

It is popular now to subscribe to the theory that this America is no more than the plunder of generations of genocidal murderers, that America's success is no more than the ill-gotten gains of three hundred years of slavery, and that the systematic rape of our natural blessings made success virtually impossible. Our stock in the history books, books we have written, has sunk below nothing and plunged to humiliation and shame. The more the federal complex can shape the common man's view of himself as a no-good killer and thief, the more we cease to be Americans and allow ourselves to be persuaded that our best self-image is that of the inhabitant of the cabbage patch: no past and no future except what Washington is willing to allow us, no liberty but what Washington believes the common man deserves, which is that of an economic unit, a slave.

This view of Americans presented by the complex, this sinister picture of the common man, is rubbish. The Promise and the Hope shaped the American character, the way that Americans traditionally want to think of themselves. This character was born in a Judeo-Christian womb and raised to value personal independence, education, family, God, and the dignity of work. America is not an accident of geography, of natural resources, or a simple run of good luck. We have been blessed with great resources, but there are vast countries and areas every bit as blessed as we have been, such as Siberia, sub-Saharan Africa, South America, and on and on, in general and in particular. Many of these places still have pre-feudal tribal societies and embrace slavery. The difference between any of those countries and ours is the common man, no more and no less. The common man grew in America, lives in America, and now is threatened by the government complex.

Following the revolution, as they wrote the Constitution and then fleshed out its workings in practice, the Founders were fond of observing that it was all new. They were acutely and at times painfully aware that each thing they did was a precedent for all that would come after. While it may have been true that it was all new, it is also true that they shared the same attributes and colonial history. None of them was seeking to establish an oriental potentate, or insisting that Muslim Sharia law would become the law of the land, or that all property be held in common. They were men and women raised speaking the same tongue and living within the confines of the same Judeo-Christian ethic that had been filtered through the English experience and poured out over this challenging new land. There were manners and class that divided them, but much more that tied them together: their language, their customs, and, most importantly, their values.

We reach the point now where there begins to be more that divides us than unites us as Americans. It is this federal complex, this Washington Establishment that seeks to separate us, to tell us how different we are from our neighbor. The complex wants splinter groups: blocs that feel dependent on the government for its largesse or its protection. The only thing that unites some portions of the population is that we happen to be living in the same country. Can it really be news to the Washington complex that nations that do not have a homogeneous population fail and split into different countries? Homogeneous does not mean that the population is all of the same race, or religion, or ethnic background. Homogeneous does mean that they speak the same language, proclaim allegiance to the same flag, and have the same basic values. A common language unites people, and separate languages separate them. It is difficult to find any western country, certainly any democracy, where there is more than one language. The closest is probably Canada with two official languages: English and French. Canada has survived with two languages, but is periodically racked with resurgent separatist movements, and it long-term viability is, at best, unclear. The Soviet Union was a country knit together from separate peoples with distinct languages, religions, and cultures. In the 1980's at its demise, the country promptly fell to fifteen separate pieces, several of whom have invaded one another. And this is after they had been pushed together for generations first by the tsars and later the commissars. To invite multiple languages, as the government complex has done, is to sow the seeds of complete and permanent dissolution.

As important as a common language is, it is not enough to keep people together in one political entity. Witness our own separation from England. While a common language may not assure a nation of success, different languages will assure it of less happiness. There is no democracy where there is a seamless amalgamation of languages. The reason for that is probably the self-evident one that without a common language, we cannot speak to one another. We have only inferential ideas of what the other person is thinking. In the end a separate-languaged people in a larger democracy are isolated and prey to special appeals. This has happened in America.

It is difficult to believe that any government would deliberately foster such policy, but the record of our own federal complex gives every indication that it wants and is willing to maintain and foster separate language populations in America. It does this under the rubric of respect for foreign and minority speakers. This policy not only virtually guarantees that the minority speakers will remain a separate economic sub-class which will have difficulty doing anything other than manual labor, but also that they can be appealed to as a separate political sub-class as the victims of those who speak the majority tongue. The question then is why would the federal government foster policies that result not just in maintaining a separate economic sub-class, but in the long term will add significant friction to maintaining us as one nation. The reason is that when the government complex pits the minority speakers against the majority speakers, the minority speakers believe that they must have a strong, robust, and growing federal government to protect them from the majority speakers. So, it is in the interest of the federal complex to ensure that there are separate education programs, separate media sources, separate political appeals, and so on for the minority speaking population. So the federal government grows larger and stronger, but at the expense of pulling apart the nation as one people. Maintaining this apartness of foreign language speakers is doubtlessly motivated by the complex' interest in maintaining them as a dependable voting bloc; the fact that this bloc is more likely to be locked into poverty and work for less money is an unintended by-product, albeit one that reinforces the self-image of the minority language speaker as dependent on the complex for protection.

So, the government complex has an interest in splintering groups that are separate from the mainstream: separate in language, separate in their identities, and who are led to feel that they must look to the federal complex for protection. But this is not in the interest of the nation. The nation's interest is to be one people regardless of our race or ethnicity. In this issue, there is a clear divergence of the interests of the federal government complex and the interests of the nation.

The culpability of the federal complex is writ large. It has refused and continues to refuse to even maintain borders to halt illegal immigration. When the border areas become infested with violence and poverty, and the local and state governments act, the federal complex brands their efforts as racist and stops the local actions through the courts. The federal government is splintering the population to promote dependence, to enhance the likelihood that that each splinter will rely on the government complex for protection against the majority speakers.

We have always been a nation of immigrants but, until recently, America has been a melting pot. For over a hundred and fifty years it was the policy of the federal government to allow and encourage immigrants from anywhere to become Americans. Gradually, after a generation or two each immigrant wave became more like the waves that preceded it. People simply thought of themselves as Americans. Moreover they wanted others to think of them simply as Americans. Not hyphenated Americans, but Americans. They may have preserved different traditions, and once or twice a year put on costumes of their grandparents' native country, but over the generations, we became alike no matter where our ancestors came from. For better or worse, one of the first foreign aspects of the immigrant to disappear was the native language. It might survive for a few generations in the home, but then it would be difficult to keep. People wanted to become this new thing: an American. And Americans spoke English.

Politicos have always recognized the value of meeting, greeting, and assisting immigrants to encourage or obligate them to support and vote for a particular party or faction. We have all read the descriptions of immigrants getting off the boat to be greeted with a cup of soup and a handshake by the party machine. But there was always the underlying assumption that these people would merge at some point into the larger America.

That assumption is no longer in vogue nor is it the policy of the federal complex. Instead, the policy encourages different ethnic and racial groups to maintain their own individual identities including language. The result has become citizens that do not think of themselves as Americans, but at most as hyphenated Americans. This is not always a matter of choice by the individuals who are hyphenated. It is not unusual now to hear Americans of European descent now called Euro-Americans by others who insist on hyphenating themselves. These hyphenated Americans have been educated by the complex to categorize Americans by race or class. These citizens have been pushed to perceive themselves as different. They have been taught by the federal complex that their differences will be used by the majority to oppress them, and only the federal complex can provide protection.

When a person describes themselves as a hyphenated American, he or she has been successfully splintered from the American mainstream. They are not Americans who happen to be black, white, brown, Protestant, Catholic, Jewish, or of Hispanic, European, or Asian descent. They are people who have been pushed to believe that they are uniquely different from other Americans, that they are unable to live or work like others because all playing fields are tilted against them, and that they must demand the protection of the federal government.

Even more than the question of language, it would seem obvious that an identifiable people that function together as a nation must share common values. Traditional American values, meaning the facets of the national character that most Americans have espoused either explicitly or implicitly since the founding of the country, are equality of all people, education, the dignity of work, and the importance of family. I am sure that there are others that can or should be added, but these will do for a start. Again, it is this federal complex that seeks to foster separation through a denigration of those values on the assumption that such a policy will develop splinter groups that promote the expansion of the control of the government.

The same intent by the federal complex to develop and foster splinter groups that is evident on the basis of language or race is also evident with values. The policy of the government is to isolate and separate out groups or segments of the population that reject one or more of the values. Frequently, encouraging the rejection of values is a tool the government complex uses to reinforce the tendency towards separation that the complex has already fostered on the basis of race or ethnicity. The federal government then appeals to and supports these groups, encourages them to believe that they are victims, and urges them to rely on the strong and growing federal government for protection.

More perfidious is that the federal complex encourages the belief that members of these splinter groups cannot compete with individuals of other ethnic or racial groups, because they have been victimized by these groups. It becomes ingrained that they need the protection of their friend, the federal government complex.

The only way the federal government complex can hold groups together as victims is to make the persons in the group believe that such factors as language and traditional American values are not important, that such ideas as family, equality, education, and the dignity of work really have no value in the modern world. The government complex moves the victim groups to believe that these values not only are of no importance, but are traps to further hold them down. It encourages the values to be ridiculed. One popular way to do this is to point out that one or more persons who espouse these values may adhere to them imperfectly and should therefore be branded as a hypocrite. The implied message then becomes that these values are being presented to further trick and deceive the victim group because the majority group itself does not adhere to them. Thus, the reason for the victim group's lack of success has nothing to do with values or language. It is instead due to overwhelming discrimination and oppression. What is important is that the victim group be portrayed as victimized by an American system dominated by and cynically used by a certain racial, economic, or ethnic group, the most popular being "white".

This rejecting of the language and values by victim groups has worked wonderfully well for the federal complex. It encourages these groups to rely on the federal complex in the belief that the federal complex is the only source for their protection which ensures their support for a more powerful complex. It gives the groups a scapegoat, a reward for being victims, and reinforces their separateness as victims. It also sets them up to fail which then reinforces their victimhood.

The federal government complex moves to obfuscate issues because the obfuscation leads to more frustration and chaos. It does not want to talk about national borders. Instead, it wants to talk about amnesty, "anchor babies", and "dream" laws. Why in the world should Americans waste breath discussing these peripheral issues until the question of the integrity of the borders is settled? How many times in the past has amnesty been debated and even granted. Nothing changed. The problem is not amnesty, nor is it babies or dreams. It is the borders. It is the federal government complex. There is nothing that will happen in the next election that will significantly change anything. The interests of the federal complex are not those of the nation. It is in the interest of the complex to develop and maintain splinter groups who believe they must rely on the federal government for protection. It is in the interest of the complex to perpetuate hyphenated Americans because these splinter groups will vote to expand the power of the federal government. It is in the interest of the federal complex to ignore national borders because that promotes chaos, destroys liberty, and assists in developing splinter groups. The interests of the complex are not the interests of America.

We vote every few years in national elections, and the appearance is given that it is the electorate that directs the federal government, but that has not been true for at least two generations and perhaps much longer. Not once did we vote to expand the budget of the federal government. Not once did we vote to let the deficit grow to ten trillion dollars. Not once did we vote to bail out AIG, or purchase General Motors. Not once did we vote to cede the southwestern states to a foreign power or to drug lords. Not once.

A more cynical system could hardly be imagined, and yet the reality is worse. The federal complex pushes the belief in the alleged oppressor groups that they are guilty of discrimination, racism, murder, slavery, rape, and extortion by the mere fact of their existence and belonging to that group. The federal complex moves forward pushing the myth that racial and ethnic splinter groups are not born free, but are born victims. Similarly the non-victim or mainstream groups are not born free, but are born guilty as the oppressors. Each group is thereby reinforced in the role that best promotes the ends of the federal complex which is to isolate groups and promote their dependence on the federal government. This is not a ploy that will be corrected when the other party comes to power or if the right candidates are elected. This is a knife wielded by the hand of the federal complex that thrusts at the very heart of America as a democracy, as a republic.

Let us pause and put this matter into perspective. In the last chapter of this book is a proposed action plan, but changing the nature of the union is a grave and serious matter. What consideration can be fraught with more peril than changing a framework that has allowed the common man the freedom to build so great a country? Changing that extraordinary union should demand extraordinary cause. That cause is no less now than it was in 1776. It is liberty, and it is life for the common man.

It is pointless to indict the governmental framework for being imperfect. It is imperfect because it was conceived and implemented by the mind of man. Perfection is too high a standard by which to judge a human institution. To argue that the nature of the union should be changed because it is imperfect is nonsense. The point of what has been laid out thus far is that a complex has developed around the legislative and executive functions of the federal government, that this complex continually pushes and drives legislation and regulation which expands the power and control of the federal government. This complex has reached a point now where the success of its efforts has dampened both the Promise and the Hope of America. The charges in the indictment are the poisonous fruit of those efforts.

Furthermore, through the successful development of splinter groups, the complex now accelerates this dampening and diminution of liberty. It is this threat and the manifestations of the threat in the indictment that cause us to say that the time has come to reconsider the nature of the union. But if the indictment was wrongly conceived, if there has been no diminution of our liberty, if the Promise and Hope are still vital, then trouble yourself no further, for there is nothing of value in the pages ahead. If you believe that these matters will or can be corrected in the next election when candidates seek their majorities, or in any following election, then work for your party and save your eyes the effort of further readings here. Certainly we can hear the retort of the federal complex: that America is a democracy and, after all, its policies and programs are the "will of the people, the majority".

CHAPTER FIVE

The Myth of the Majority

We are a democracy and democracies generally bow to the will of a majority. Being ruled by a majority vote has a nice ring to it, one to which we have grown accustomed and which seems to contain its own legitimacy. It is the basis for democracy. We have been taught since our earliest age that there is something almost sacred about a majority. It is the "will of the people". The one who frustrates the will of the people is a scoundrel and a tyrant. One of our traditional charges against communism is that no communist party has ever been voted to power by a majority of a nation's populace. Anything with the stamp of the "majority" is considered sacrosanct. So how can we seriously contemplate changing the nature of the union when such an action may not be supported by a majority of people throughout the country?

To address that question, begin by looking at the nature of democracy and voting in America. Our nation has generally striven towards the principle that one person has one vote and that vote is equal to all other persons' votes. That is the basis of a democracy for a free and equal people. Yet we know that in practice each vote does not always have equal weight. The vote of a person for a senatorial candidate in a state with a small population does not carry the same weight as the vote of a person in a state with a large population. The same is even true for congressional districts because the populations are never really the same. Then we consider such matters as the difficulty a person may have voting because it is more convenient here and less convenient there. It will never come out entirely equal simply because we are human and we are entitled to some slack. The point is that although we strive towards the ideal of one equal vote for each person, there are some limitations because of the simple fact that we are not perfect. It would not be fair to attack our voting process if this were the only basis for doing so.

We should also bear in mind that we are not a true democracy. The classic example of a true democracy is the Greek city states where each person qualified to vote could vote directly on an issue. The difference in our system is that although we call ourselves a democracy, we are more accurately a republic. We do not vote on issues ourselves, with the possible exception of an occasional local or statewide referendum.

Instead, the voters elect representatives to federal office who then vote on behalf of their constituency. The representative thus represents thousands or millions of voters. Many of the constituents may not like or want this representative, but on a given day, election day, at least one half of the voters plus one voted for that person to represent them and, presumably, the policies which that candidate espoused. In fact, in some American elections, when the anti-incumbency mood of the people has been strong, the voting for the winning candidate may have been influenced more by disliking the other candidate rather than supporting the winner. A winning representative may go to Washington without any substantial support among his constituents. This would almost always be true when the election cycle and other factors result in a low turnout.

Then there is the practice of "gerrymandering", the art and the science whereby the political party in power draws up new districts wherein their candidates stand the best chance of winning elections, or at least the greatest numbers of their candidates stand the best chance of winning, even if they may have to sacrifice a district here or there. While gerrymandering is always deplored by the party not in power, who are itching to do the same thing themselves when they are back on top, the actual outcome may or may not result in districts where the elected representative is more likely to reflect the views of his or her constituents. In fact, argument can be made that gerrymandering enhances the ability of a republic to reflect the will of its population. Alternatively it can be fairly argued that gerrymandering results in the opposite: less effective representation. An example is where a district that is overwhelmingly of one persuasion is divided so that smaller groups can tip the scales in several other districts and result in a greater number of representatives of that particular party being elected. In a true democracy, like the old Greek city-states, there is no gerrymandering because each citizen votes directly; it only becomes an issue in a republic such as ours.

These practices complicate the issue of determining what constitutes a legitimate majority. However, these are imperfections in our system that result from our striving to have elections that carry that certain flavor of legitimacy required to be swallowed and accepted by us, the people. While not desirable in an idealized state, we know that we will always fall short of an ideal for the simple reason that we are human, less than perfect. An acceptable democracy becomes a matter of degree. It becomes a matter of how many imperfections can be accepted before the system is simply unacceptable, before the citizens say that the results of the election are not legitimate. Over time we have been fortunate to have avoided practices that undermine elections such as outright fraud in voting and counting of ballots. We have protected the integrity of the actual voting. Sure, the party in power throws its weight around and gerrymanders a district here or there, but in the next cycle it will be re-gerrymandered, and, frankly, it is hard to tell whether it is a good thing or a bad thing.

But now, democracy and voting in America has been compromised and undercut by the federal government complex. It has done this by developing voting blocs, or splinter groups. The complex has created, developed, and protected these splinter groups who have been encouraged to believe that they must rely on the federal complex for protection. They have been successfully split off from the main body of the electorate. The traditional splinter groups have been based on race, religion, or ethnicity. A group is successfully splintered when two things occur. The first is that the federal complex enacts measures to reinforce the identity of the group by offering special protections or rewards. The second is that the group responds by thinking of themselves as a distinct group and by voting as a bloc for the expansion of the complex control. In any election the political commentators all discuss various segmented voters. These may be the "white vote", the "black vote", the "middle class vote", the "senior vote", the "eighteen to twenty-five vote", the "Catholic vote", the "blue collar vote" and so on. The appeal of any particular candidate to the various segments is analyzed and projected by commentators and put on colored charts and maps to enhance digestion.

Any segment is a potential splinter group. However, simply being an identifiable segment of the population with identifiable political leanings does not make a splinter group. A real splinter group requires cultivation. There must be laws or regulations enacted that either protect or appear to protect and reward that group, and the splinter group itself must respond. It maintains its identity as a group which needs these protections or rewards. The protection or reward tends to reinforce that group's identity and separateness. The complex can then rely on this group to want to expand the power and the control of the complex because that group's identity has been reinforced, and its members see their well-being as intimately tied to the well-being of the federal government. They see the expansion of control as a positive development because they view their own well-being as thus expanding. The interplay between the complex and the splinter group becomes mutually reinforcing.

A splinter group is built on the idea of inequality. Splintering both relies on perceived inequality and reinforces perceived inequality. The federal complex encourages splintering and the consequent feeling of separateness. It is a cynical and vicious ploy that continues in practice because it works: the splinter groups always support an expansion of the federal government's control and the consequent diminution in liberty. It has been called the Balkanization of America; the reduction of the American people into separate hyphenated tribes that are no longer a nation.

Splintering has generally used race or ethnicity as the basis for the group. But now in the first decade of the twenty-first century, America has seen an expansion of that concept to include employees of certain entities as well as unions. In the recent recession the federal government stepped into the economy and actually bought or seized a failed car company, General Motors. The complex injected tens of billions of dollars into that company to keep it on life support. General Motors had been led by its board of directors to financial doom. It was unable to effectively compete in the free market. The free market's solution was simple: the company must close or shrink and its assets sold off for value. It happens every day to hundreds of companies that are unable to compete. When the federal complex stepped in and gave General Motors these billions of dollars to keep it functioning, it created a new splinter group based on employment. The board of directors and employees of General Motors learned that the best way to keep their jobs is not by making automobiles and trucks, but by voting for a vibrant, healthy, successful, and expanding federal government. Money does not need to constantly flow to General Motors from the federal government each year; the knowledge that it is available and will be used is sufficient. The federal complex has thus changed the Promise and the Hope of

America into a promise and hope of a bailout if and only if the complex keeps growing. This issue of the federal complex subverting the free market economy is so important that it will be discussed further in later chapters because when the free market ceases to exist, so will any semblance of liberty. However, here is the simpler point that the federal complex expanding the concept of splinter groups from those based on race or ethnicity to a splinter group based on employment.

Compare this with the "Cash for Clunkers" program that stimulated the sales of automobiles in this country. The net affect of this program was to give Americans a discount if they purchased a vehicle, said discount being a gift from the taxpayer. While this program did stimulate the sale of motor vehicles, it did not create splinter groups. From the perspective of the federal complex, the General Motors bailout was a far wiser move. Not only did it blaze new territory in terms of direct involvement with the economy, but it set up new splinter groups. For the complex it was a win-win-win situation. Even though the federal government may seek to lessen its direct ownership of General Motors, the splinter group is a lasting affect and benefit to the federal complex.

So let us now re-consider the legitimacy of a majority. The question is a simple one. Is it possible to have a fair election where there are splinter groups? Does a manufactured majority carry the same legitimacy as a non-manufactured majority? Let me ask the question a different way: do we accept the equality of man or do we not? The federal complex, this Washington Establishment, this aura of power, despite its fine rhetoric and its chiseled writings, seeks inequality for in inequality there are splinter groups and there is power.

In America equality is an issue that at times in our history has literally bled us white. It was a principle set forth in the Declaration of Independence and which nearly resulted in our stillbirth as country. Time and again in our nation's youth the acceptance of equality as a principle, but inequality as a practice, nearly tore us apart. In the 1860's the matter could be glossed over no longer. Our acceptance not just of the principle of the equality of man but also the practice was settled at a tremendous price paid in blood and material well-being.

One hundred years later the nation confronted the Jim Crow laws which, if they did not reestablish a pale semblance of slavery, at least held people of color in a second class citizenship. But for at least the past fifty years Americans of color, among others, have also been a prime target for splintering tactics. Still other groups that have traditionally been targets of discrimination have not responded as splinter groups even though they have been offered specific protections by the complex. The largest and most notable is women. Women are not a splinter group because while they may have welcomed the protection, they have refused to respond as a predictable and cohesive group.

In this nation's history every wave of immigrants has had to contend with stereotyping, profiling, and discrimination. Each wave has managed to overcome their initially inferior social and economic status with sufficient success so as to look down their noses at the next wave. This has been true with every single wave of immigrants regardless of their nationality, religion, race, or color. I do not suggest that it was easy, that it was fair, or to minimize their struggle. I state only that whatever hardships they faced, it was better here in America where they had the liberty to roll their dice on a relatively flat table. We know that is true because they kept coming and very few ever returned whence they came. Until recently they achieved success without the assistance of federal laws mandating that they be treated in a certain manner.

Remember though that it is in the interest of the federal complex that identifiable splinter groups not achieve success, not merge into the mainstream of American life. It is better that they be pointed to as victims of discrimination in housing, employment, education, and every other facet of American life and that specific programs be designed to alleviate the inequality. In the past all those programs have done is to continue to reinforce the perception of these groups as permanently enfeebled and dependent on the government's largesse and protection. Look at the ghettos and barrios that have existed generation after generation. The federal complex calls it "ethnic pride", but it might better be termed "the new slavery". These splinter groups became and remain an identifiable and dependable voting bloc to promote the growth of the government and the shrinking of individual liberty. Not only do these laws and programs promote the separateness of the splinter group by encouraging the splinter group members to think of themselves as separate, but they cannot help but arouse resentment among everyone who is not a member of that splinter group by the seeming favored treatment. So the federal complex wins from two directions.

Aside from the political argument that this weakens the nation as a democracy, it is morally wrong for the government complex to take any group of people and encourage them to remain as a splintered group of second class and dependent citizens. To do it in hopes that this group will assist the government complex to undercut liberty is a cynical outrage.

In so doing the federal government complex cheapens the liberty of its citizens. The complex cannot change. It cannot correct. The concept of a majority has less legitimacy when there are significant portions of the electorate that have become splinter groups. This is not going to be corrected in the next election. There are no candidates running on the platform of equality and ending the use by the federal complex of race, ethnicity, religion, sex, country of origin, and, now, employer to create splinter groups. Ironically, for a candidate to run on a platform of equality would invite charges of racism, political incorrectness, and un-Americanism.

What a mess! The Promise and the Hope lay bleeding and battered, but to point it out is both racist and subversive. The result is that our elections become compromised and one can fairly question whether they any longer reflect the judgments of a free people.

This process of Balkanization will only exacerbate the symptoms further. Remember the metaphor of the sailing ship being blown towards the rocks: the wind only blows in one direction, towards more control and loss of liberty. It is not a matter of changing a few laws and drawing back on spending. This wind will continue to blow and any temporary gains will be lost because the complex is still there and the splinter groups are still splintered. This sounds like a hopeless scenario wherein liberty in America is doomed. That is not true, but there must be a counterbalance to the power of the complex and its willingness to subvert our democracy and tear us apart as a nation. Fortunately, the institutions that can become a counterbalance already exist: the states. This is really a message of promise and hope, a message that echoes down to us from 1776.

It was the states, the colonies, which created the federal government. They did so to enhance and protect the welfare of its citizens. But now this federal complex threatens to consume Americans from the inside, to "eat out their Substance" as Jefferson wrote about appointed officials many years ago. The states still have the power to rein in the complex and protect their citizens. The only question is whether the will to do so can be re-instilled into the state capitols. There is no balance now between the states and the federal government as the Founders intended. Instead the power has shifted completely over to the federal government with the states reduced to the role of handmaidens. It is time to change. It is high time. When that change begins, the federal complex will respond that its way is the way of the majority, that America is a democracy and the majority rules. Remember then that it was the complex that created that majority, that it was the complex that took these splintered Americans and told them that they were different, told them that they could not succeed on their own, that bought their votes as surely as if it had stuffed their pockets with cash. So when the federal complex responds that its will is the will of the majority, you will know that it is a majority that the complex created.

"For imposing Taxes on us without our Consent."
The Declaration of Independence, 1776

CHAPTER SIX

Money and No Money

Dollars will be thrown about in the next few pages, so keep your head down because these dollars are big and they are ugly. The numbers are in billions and trillions, so many zeros that we write "one billion" instead of 1,000,000,000 because the human eye does not gladly contemplate that many zeros. One billion is a one followed by nine zeros, and one trillion is a one followed by twelve zeros. These numbers are so big that they have no real meaning, so let us try to put them into some kind of perspective. There are about three hundred million people in America. That is a three followed by a mere eight zeros. If we wanted the federal government to spend one billion dollars this year, each one of us would have to kick in about three dollars and thirty three cents. So for every multiple of one billion dollars, each man, woman, and child has to kick in the same multiple of three dollars and thirty three cents. Three bucks is a pretty good deal, and remember that it was not much more than one hundred years ago that the federal budget crossed this one billion dollar mark. But let us say that we wanted federal spending to be one trillion dollars. That is one thousand billions of dollars or about three thousand three hundred and thirty three dollars that each person would have to kick in.

To make it simpler, let us imagine that the average family in America is four persons: Ma, Pa, Junior, and Sis. That means that our average family is kicking in about thirteen thousand three hundred dollars for every trillion dollars that we want the federal government to spend. Let us move directly to the punch line. Early in 2010 the national debt was approximately 12.3 trillion dollars. That means that our average American family is actually in debt to the tune of one hundred and sixty four thousand dollars. Not once, not one time did anyone in the family vote to take on that debt. Instead, it was officially given to them by their elected representatives in the executive and legislative branches of the federal government; the debt is a gift to the family from the majority, the "will of the people". That sum is staggering. In most areas of this country that family could buy a pretty nice house for themselves.

In 2008 the national debt reached a milestone: for the first time in history it increased by a solid one trillion dollars in a single year. That means the federal government spent one trillion dollars more than it took in through taxes. For the fiscal years 2003 through 2007 the federal government was spending about one dollar and twenty cents for every dollar it took in; in 2009 it spent one dollar and ninety cents for every dollar it received. The deficit for 2010 is expected to add another 1.3 trillion dollars to the debt.

Our national debt is not interest free. During the 2009 fiscal year we paid out about 189 billion dollars in interest. Our little four person family had to kick in another $2,520 to cover that interest, or would have had to except that the government just borrowed it and added the interest to the deficit. These are real dollars that are going into someone's pocket, and about half of those someones speak Mandarin. The year before the amount was $242 billion, but the government, like the rest of us, benefited in 2009 from the lower interest rates. Remember that this is just interest on the debt, and does not repay one cent of the 12.3 trillion principal. On top of that interest payment is another interest expense commonly called intra-governmental interest. That is the interest that the government theoretically pays itself when it "borrows" from funds that have a surplus, like social security. The government is basically promising to repay the money that it borrowed from one fund and spent in another area, and promising to pay interest as well. That intra-governmental interest amounted to another 192 billion. Although that interest is calculated into the national debt, it is really a non-number because anyone who believes that the federal government is going to pay interest on the money it has taken from Social Security is nuts, but it keeps the books neat.

Then came the recession of 2008-2010. The government spent hundreds of billions of dollars buying up bad debt and underwriting bankrupt companies. It committed 120 billion to AIG alone. That 120 billion is a twelve followed by ten zeros. Let's print out all those zeros to see if the numbers look smaller: 120,000,000,000. No, they don't look smaller. That comes out to $1,600 for our family of four. That's you; that's me; it's the guy next door who lost his job; it's the family down the street who lost their home. The government complex, the Washington Establishment, put over sixteen hundred dollars onto my family's back and your family's back so that the incompetents and scoundrels in AIG could be made whole. Imagine what a tremendous stimulant to the economy would have occurred if the government had given that money back to the taxpayers who gave the money to the government in the first place. AIG, the banks, the investment houses have all learned that if they can figure out how to gamble with trillions of dollars instead of millions, they can keep any gain, but "federalize" any losses or risk. The buzz phrase was "too big to fail". Keeping gain but transferring risk was the dream of every nineteenth century robber baron and twentieth century market plunderer, and we have lived to see their humble dream come true. It should make the old pirates want to put on lederhosen and run across a mountaintop singing "The hills are alive...".

You may hear that all of this is just numbers, that it has no meaning to the average guy or his family: people like our Ma, Pa, Junior, and Sis. If that is true, tell Ma and Pa to subtract out from this year's tax bill the $1,600 that the federal complex forced their family to give to AIG. Do you think that the IRS will agree that the money has no meaning, or do you think that Ma's and Pa's wages will be garnished before they go to prison?

Trillions of dollars were used by the complex to buy up bad debt, these toxic assets, and to underwrite losses and guarantee risk. The Federal Reserve alone guaranteed nine trillion dollars in loans in domestic and foreign banks. When the government complex underwrites risk for the financial houses, who do you think the complex is committing to pay out losses? Is it the scammers on Wall Street or is it the common man? Do not confuse this with the policies of the Democrats or the policies of the Republicans. It is both, it is the federal complex. The complex creates the conditions for the chaos from which it grows and benefits. In the course of a few months in 2008 and

2009 every family of four allowed the biggest losers in business world history to transfer tens of thousands of dollars' worth of debt and risk onto their backs and the backs of their children. Can you read this and seriously contend that your rights to life, liberty, and the pursuit of happiness are still intact?

The government will have to pay its debt in one of three ways. The first is raising taxes to repay the debt over the course of the next umpteen years. The complex will not move towards that because it is not even willing to pay the interest now. The interest is itself thrown on top of the ten trillion each year to create even more debt. Rather than raise taxes, the government complex could cut spending drastically, and we can expect that to happen soon after they stop shoving pork and earmarks into the budget, which is to say never. The second way to pay the debt is simply to print more money and pay it off. That sounds easy, but dollar for dollar the debt would return to us as inflation. If we paid the debt off today by printing the money needed to cover it and giving that to the lenders, aside from the fact the lenders would be infuriated, every dollar we now have would be worth about fifty cents. It would be as though the government took one of every two dollars you have or dollars you earn, using the balance to pay off the debt. The third way is a variant of the first: hope that in some future years the government will have an excess of revenue over expenses and be able to use that money to pay off the debt. In 2000 the economy had actually expanded to the point where this was seen as possible over the course of the next decade or so.

The usual explanation is that with the bursting of the dot-com bubble in 2002 and the massive increase in government spending in the next half-dozen years, that scenario had become a pipe dream and disappeared like so much smoke. That is the explanation, but the driving force that buried the excess revenue in debt was the federal complex. To expand its control into the economy and into the life of the common man, the complex needs chaos and deficits. That is what fills campaign coffers, creates opportunity to propose and oppose legislation, and expands the business of governance. So the excess revenues rapidly became a deficit, and with the recession of 2008, the common man was drowning.

Some economists project that increased revenues from an expanding economy in the years ahead, maybe forty percent of the debt may disappear. This does not involve magic. It still means that instead of having an excess in the future, today's deficit is still being paid out of future revenues. We will be less healthy later. The government complex has experts and consultants, economists and accountants with charts and graphs, who glibly give the impression that somehow tomorrow's prosperity washes out today's excess by some sleight of hand. It is not true. The common man will pay off that debt. He will do so by having his currency devalued or by paying more taxes later.

Well might one ask how this squares with a government established by the several States with the express purpose of promoting the "general Welfare". The federal complex does not care whether or not the common man is hoodwinked or bled dry. Within the complex there are umpteen foundations, commissions, mini-movements, politicos, and funded studies dedicated to "fiscal responsibility", whatever that means, and balancing this or that budget, or some spending caps. If these groups ever reached their goals and the government was put on a permanent balanced budget, they would be out of business. They would have to fold up shop and go look for work elsewhere; they would have failed. Their experts and consultants would join the ranks of the unemployed. The federal complex needs chaos and irresponsibility in the system if it is to thrive and grow. That is why it does not matter if the government does achieve some level of financial success, as it did in the late 90's, the federal complex will not allow it to continue. It needs deficits, chaos, and uncertainty if it is to thrive. Only the states can stop this, and they can do it by standing up for their citizens and saying "No".

The federal government has not been the only ones with financial pipe dreams. Many state governments leaped onto the debt wagon. The individual state, like the federal government, spent more without raising revenues. The difference between the debt accumulated by the state governments and the debt accumulated by the federal government is that the states do not have all of the options available for repayment that the federal government has: specifically the ability to print money and water down the currency. However, the states do have an extra option: looking to the federal government for assistance. The federal government can take on the debt of the state governments by providing funds to meet the state deficits and enable them generally to continue in operation. This sounds like a reasonable approach for the deficit states, in fact, it probably sounds like a fantastic solution to their high spending legislators. The federal government will get that money from taxing, printing, or borrowing. It takes the deficit state's debt and spreads it out to every person living in America. For example, the state of California recently estimated a twenty five billion dollar deficit in their budget. Using the three hundred million population number, this comes out to eighty three dollars for everyone. After looking at some of the other numbers, the cost of bailing out California is peanuts. We should jump on it; what a great deal!

However, there are two ugly little problems that stick up their warty heads when the federal government assists states with their deficits. The first is that whatever is driving the deficit in a state's budget is going to remain to cause deficits in the future. Assistance from the federal government is only a temporary fix, or at least should be temporary. In fact, that assistance may actually push the state into greater irresponsibility. Rather than face the tough choices of bringing its spending into line with its income, the state may prefer to continue on its way with a little window dressing for the folks at home in the belief that the federal government will step in again when danger threatens. Another reason for not fixing their problem is that the state's bond rating will improve if it is apparent that the federal government will stand behind the state. That then encourages more borrowing to meet the operational deficit. So, the federal government's assistance may actually counter whatever efforts there may be in the state legislature to move towards a balanced budget.

The second problem with the federal government bailing out a particular state is equity. Should every man, woman, and child in America pay for California's deficit? Unless they live in California, it is unlikely that they received any benefit, although nobody in California except for a beloved few may have received much benefit either. California went out partying. Now that the bill is coming due, the hope is that you and your family in Iowa, Nebraska, or the Carolinas will let them use your charge card.

It is as though your neighbor threw a great party to which you were not invited, but then expects you to chip in and pay for it. You ask him why, and he tells you that you have this obligation because you live on the same block, and, after all, "we are all in this together". And not only that, but he tells you that he expects to throw another big party next year.

What will happen, in fact has happened, is that the federal complex will give money to the states with deficits, but will do so in disguise. The federal complex claims it is giving the money to the strapped states so that they will not have to fire their teachers. That is like your partying neighbor telling you that the money you are going to give him is not going to be used for the party, but for his children's shoes. Are you going to deny his children having shoes? Oh, by the way, you are not invited to next year's party either.

Why would one government, the federal government, take on the obligations of another governmental entity, in this instance, that of a state? The answer is that from the perspective of the federal complex, it is a good move. It expands the complex's base, creates dependence by states and particularly those sectors of the states' budgets that are feeling threatened. That would almost certainly be the service sector employees such as policemen, teachers, or healthcare workers. These are immense groups of voters that can be brought under the aegis of the federal complex. They become splinter groups, the same as those that the federal complex creates from ethnic, racial, or religious groups, except that what glues them together is that their jobs would be cut, or their salaries or benefits reduced without the federal largesse, even though the federal assistance might be a relatively small portion of the total wages and benefits. That creates large blocs of state employees who are groomed to expect and to rely on the largesse of the federal complex, and who can be expected to support the complex as it moves into other areas of the economy. The complex gets a much bigger bang for its buck by giving money to the states when the money directly targets these groups, rather than simply putting dollars into the states' general coffers. Moreover it is much more saleable to the public at large to pontificate that the federal money is to keep the schools open or for public safety. Simply putting money into the states' general coffers creates dependence, but it does not create the financially dependent splinter group. These splinter groups become the tool that will accelerate the success and growth of the complex.

From the perspective of the federal complex creating dependence is a progressive move. The federal complex does not care about deficits. In fact if it had to choose between deficits and no deficits, the complex picks deficits because deficits create dependence on government action. We can look at the complex and not see this because its purposes and incentives are so counterintuitive to that of the individual or even what we expect from a government that seeks "to promote the general Welfare". The federal complex moves always towards power and control through legislation and regulation. To do so, it seeks to separate and splinter Americans, not unite them. It seeks to create indefinite dependence on the complex by any group that it can splinter on any demographic basis including financial. Deficit budgets and debts are to be encouraged because they create this dependence. People are encouraged to spend foolishly in their personal lives because this tends to create dependence on government programs. The complex welcomes threats, both internal and external, and it seeks more chaos because those are the times when it can expect its power to grow.

A state that is dependent on meeting the shortfalls in its own budget with money from the federal complex will never, under any circumstances, protect its citizens from the federal complex. Although the states are the best hope of protecting the liberty of the common man, states which have become dependent on the largesse of the complex will not stand, will not counterbalance. For them there is only further complicity, growing dependence, and the ultimate loss of liberty for their citizens.

CHAPTER SEVEN

Money and Power

Money and power are like love and marriage, or at least like love and marriage were supposed to be in the old song: together. This is true for any mature government. Interestingly, they do not always go together in a new revolutionary government as it forms. We saw this with our own Founders in the 1780's, in France in the 1790's, and in the communist take-overs in the last century. Money is not a motivator for revolutionary leaders and they are never very good with it. Money issues may have set the stage for their revolution in the form of terrible inequities, but not always. Again, look at our own experience. Revolutionary leaders may later succumb to Mammon and drain the country dry, but that is another story.

Generally, a new form of government has to settle down before it attracts the money interests and those interested in the money interests. That is because, as the economists tell us, money likes stability. Capital flows towards stability and away from turmoil. At the successful conclusion of a revolution, there is usually a lot of fun to be had tearing down this or that statue, or executing the old gang, but sooner or later the revolutionaries want to build something, anything, and that takes capital. Money. When they cannot get capital, bad things happen as we will see with Russia in the 1920's. That may have been an instance of bad things happening and, therefore, no capital, but capital is not particularly choosy. It just wants stability. In the long run, and even the short run for that matter, money likes power and power likes money.

In America, there has been the worry that money would corrupt power. Occasionally it has corrupted legislators for their votes, or regulators for favorable treatment. It is a theme that arises periodically, but our track record with corruption is both amazing and enviable. Despite occasional problems and problem areas, America has been, by and large, free of corruption. We do not particularly even like going to foreign countries where baksheesh is a way of life and is expected. This stability has been a key factor to America's economic success.

But America's problem now is not money corrupting power, but of power corrupting money. Power corrupting money sounds impossible, doesn't it, but in America nothing is impossible. In 1961 Kennedy told the world that Americans would be on the moon by the end of the decade. It sounded impossible, but in 1969 Armstrong walked on the lunar surface. And forty years later we figured out how power could corrupt money. Nothing stops us when we put our mind to it.

The federal complex is encouraging the concentration of money into certain companies and organizations, and dependence by those companies on the federal complex. Through that dependence the federal complex will control the economy. Certain companies and commercial entities are favored by the government complex because of their size. These include AIG, Citicorp, the large teachers' and automotive unions, and General Motors. Since 2008 we can discern favored entities because taxpayer money underwrote massive losses that these entities generated through bad judgment, greed, and incompetence. The amounts of money that was either given outright to the companies or put at risk to guarantee their solvency is staggering. If the money given to AIG alone was the GDP of a country, that country would have a larger GDP than Vietnam or the Ukraine, and only slightly smaller than that of New Zealand or Hungary. Not one single voter cast a ballot for these monies to be used in this manner. In fact I would defy the government complex to find a single voter whose opinion was even sought.

There is the pervasive feeling that Wall Street has little to do with real life. Large companies are represented there as they have always been, but the sense now is that the markets in general, and Wall Street in particular, are run for the protected insiders, those being cultivated by the federal complex who are making the money at the expense of the average investor and taxpayer. In fact it is more than just a sense; it is what is actually happening. The taxpayer is now required to contribute money to make up losses for the favored companies. Yes, Wall Street is doing very well, thank you. The problem for Americans is that Wall Street no longer reflects what is going on in the real economy, and by that I mean what is going on in people's lives, how well the average American is doing. We know that the large banks and investment houses are going gangbusters, but Americans were not worried about them in the first place. However, the federal complex does worry about them, and when they tanked, the complex stepped in to underwrite the losses. While the complex was handing out blank checks to these criminals, unemployment was heading over ten percent, and the actual number of unemployed was closer to eighteen percent. If you see how Wall Street reflects the condition of the common man, please point it out to me, to someone, to anyone.

Wall Street serves Wall Street. That is the way it should be because America has a free market. But to force Americans to underwrite Wall Street is a betrayal of the liberty of the common man. It is stealing from him. Had one state the courage to have stood up for its citizens and said "No", this theft would not have occurred. Do not look to Washington to correct Washington because it cannot do so.

These banks and investment houses are not building America, or bringing jobs to Americans. The best that can be said for them is that they provide the loans to those who do build America. This is an essential function in a free market; capital is the gasoline in the economic engine. But it is not the engine. The only thing the banks are building and bringing is profits to themselves. There is nothing wrong with that; after all, making profits is the American way. What is wrong is that the government complex is now willing to guarantee their profits and underwrite their losses. The government complex has now fixed the system so that for these financial houses; there is no risk. The government complex has transferred the risk to the average American, the common man. What kind of government would do such a thing? It is a government and government complex that is going to control the economy and for whom your personal liberty is no hurdle.

Look at what has happened in the last forty years to our common man. Even as the average worker productivity has surged in the last three decades, hourly wages have stagnated. At the same time the incomes of the elite have gone through the stratosphere. Between 1973 and 2003 the real GDP per capita increased seventy three percent. That means that our worker productivity increased by that amount in thirty years in real dollars. That is a national success, a shout-from-the-rooftops hurrah for the common man. However, before you celebrate too hard, know that the real median hourly compensation increased only thirteen percent during those thirty years. That is a national shame, a scandal. Despite gains in productivity, despite a stock market that has more than doubled and re-doubled again, the average American worker is barely ahead.

Have there been gains in the standard of living for families? Undeniably, yes. Let's see how those gains came to be. In 1960 the percentage of Americans who were working was 37.8, but by 2008 that number had increased to 48.3. The gains to families have come at the expense of putting both adults in the family to work. So in the last thirty or forty years the rich have gotten richer and the middle class, the common man, has worked harder. Much harder. This is not a recipe for a workable democracy. It looks as though the middle class is doing better, but it is the proverbial smoke and mirrors. The household gains have been made by putting two breadwinners in the marketplace instead of one. And now we find that not only do the very rich get richer, but that the government complex is willing to transfer risk away from them to the common man and wealth to them from the common man. What a tragedy for a great country.

The complex views human beings as economic units to be milked and bilked, and occasionally led to polling places to vote in meaningless elections. No longer can just one working

American expect to support a family in a middle class lifestyle. The average work week was set at forty hours over half a century ago. Despite these enormous gains in productivity the average work week is still forty hours. So not only has the American worker made no real gains for forty years despite soaring productivity, not only has another adult in the American household had to go into the workplace to hang on to a middle class lifestyle, but the common man now also has the privilege of working longer and harder than virtually anywhere else in the West. How can we have allowed a well ordered government formed "to promote the general Welfare" to do this to the common man, to you and me? I can almost hear at least one well-known commentator screaming "class warfare" or that Americans work so hard because they have a "passion", or should have a passion, for their jobs. Bullshit. The standard of living in America should be increasing to reflect the productivity of the nation. The hours that an American works should be decreasing to allow more time for family, education, or going fishing. To treat the citizenry as though we have no more dignity than beasts of burden is appalling. If this is class warfare, then let it be so. It was precipitated by the federal complex as it moved to concentrate wealth to facilitate control. It was declared by the federal complex as it restricted the liberty of the common man to reduce him to an economic unit.

Do not answer the question of "how this could have happened" with "those damn Republicans" or "those idiot Democrats". It is neither; it is both. It makes no difference who is in power; it makes no difference for whom you vote. To the government complex the dignity of the common man has no more substance than the vote you cast in the last election. The government complex has goals and expectations that are different from the citizenry. The complex moves to develop more control of the citizenry no matter who is elected, no matter what party is in power.

Before going further, understand that the government complex is not really anti-middle class or pro-wealthy. In the end the complex is class neutral. It simply and always moves towards control. The path to control is easiest through control of the economy. The path is easier if the complex can concentrate the wealth. It is easier still if the complex finds a bottleneck like controlling the currency through banks and the Federal Reserve. In a later chapter we will explore how the exercise of human rights is tied to a free market economy: that neither will exist without the other. The federal complex is moving to control the economy by encouraging the concentration of capital. We see that unfolding in the slogan "too big to fail".

Now, we come to the crux of why there is a pervasive sense in America that our children will not have it better. This great hope of every generation is reaching an end. There may still be breath in the hope of the working poor to rise into the middle class, but the promise and expectation that the common man's life will improve from generation to generation is gasping.

The government complex has made clear that if an entity controls or owns a certain level of assets, then it can expect that the taxpayer will underwrite any losses or overextensions. The government complex is encouraging capital to mass and then underwrites losses. The government complex thus begins to control the financial market. The market forces of capitalism cease to work. Instead of the usual and customary route for failure, which is bankruptcy and dispersal of its assets, the federal complex saves these firms which, in turn, encourages further mergers and massing of capital. So there is an actual trade-off. The massed capital is dependent on the government complex which is in a position to control the economic life of the country. In turn, the massed capital wins no matter what losses its policies and decisions generate. In fact the greater the losses, the greater the dependence.

This is wonderful for the individuals who control the massed capital. They can keep the gains, but any losses are underwritten by the citizens. There was considerable thunder in the media when these individuals received enormous bonuses from their companies, sometimes tens of millions of dollars, despite the fact that under their leadership the companies had completely failed and would have been bankrupt if they had not been bailed out. However, one might argue that these individuals not only deserved those bonuses, but even more because they had placed their companies in the hitherto unattainable position in a supposedly free market economy of a completely risk-free position. Their hope of gain is no longer restrained by their fear of loss. Not only should these individuals and boards of directors have received immense bonuses, they should have had statues of themselves erected, perhaps around the capitol dome in Washington.

The identity of interest between those amassing capital and the Federal Reserve is breathtaking in its arrogance. How often have we heard politicos tell us that the justification for the Reserve continuing to exist and remain independent of the political process is that it removes monetary and economic policy from the politicos who might be tempted to use it for political ends? So our representatives are telling us that although they do not trust themselves or their judgment, they still have complete faith in their ability to represent the common man, and hope that you and I will elect them again. Is this making sense to anyone? Do you still have faith in your vote to affect the course of the country in the next election?

It is difficult to maintain the facade that America has a free market economy that winnows out the losers when in practice the federal complex protects preferred entities by filling in any losses with money from the taxpayer, or guarantees backed by the current taxpayers' children and grandchildren.

This initiative by the government complex is an absolutely unparalleled expansion of power. It brings us closer to a managed economy, and destroys the advantages of the competitive free market system. These companies no longer need to compete in any real sense. In fact, their best strategic move is to merge and become larger, and thereby control still more assets. This is happening now with the banks and financial firms. It is success through acquisition and dependence on the government complex, not through competition.

This is not just a purist's complaint or a taxpayer's grouch. The action by the government complex dampens the free market and its system of rewards and losses. It is the free market system and competition that has enabled America to reach its level of economic success and superiority. Had there not been bail-outs, there certainly would have been pain in the economy that would have been felt world-wide, and the pain no doubt would have been more immediate than what there was after the bail-outs, but we would have gotten through that pain and then moved on. The government could have and should have assisted Americans in stimulating the economy and adjusting to the fallout. However, the action that was taken by the government complex will now give us greater economic pain, and put America in a disadvantageous position in the long term.

It is as though in the late nineteenth century the government had met with the buggy manufacturers and given them money to upgrade their products, build new plants, and underwritten whatever losses they were experiencing due to the advent of the automobile. That might have worked for a while. Certainly there were entire communities and families that had provided a skilled service for generations who were being driven out of business. The government might have encouraged them to merge together into one immense corporation. These activities could have discouraged the development of any automobile industry at all in America, particularly if the government built in some tax disincentives. It could have worked for a decade, maybe even for a generation. Instead of developing here, the auto industry either never would have developed as it did, or, more likely, would have emerged in other countries.

But everyone always picks on the poor buggy manufacturers. Let us look at a more recent example: computers. In the 40's and early 50's computers were monstrous affairs with hundreds or thousands of vacuum tubes. Even the engineers developing the computers could not imagine that more than a few dozen would ever be needed in the United States and these few would be owned by entities like the IRS, entities with massive volumes of data or that needed complex calculations. It simply was not imagined that computers could be useful in other circumstances. Moreover unions, factories, employees, and communities had enormous investments in continuing to design, make, and manufacture the mechanical devices such as electric typewriters and adding machines that are now in the town dump or museums. Cutting edge technology at the time was an electric typewriter that could erase itself. It would have been easy in a controlled and dependent economy to adhere to the original concept of a few computers, and to avoid the dislocation and disruption that computers caused throughout the economy. Maintaining the status quo would have satisfied virtually everyone, but a free market does not care about satisfying the status quo. Some country that allowed the free market to work sooner or later would have developed these computers. It might have been Western Europe, China, or India. Or, unlikely as it may seem, it might have been the North Koreans. However comfortable we would have been for a few years, maybe even a generation or two, that comfort would have ended uncomfortably.

It can be so easy to discourage new innovations and new technologies. The government would do so in a managed economy because new technology disrupts the system. In the 70's and early 80's engineers had brought the electric typewriter to a state of near functional perfection. Computer use for word processing was clumsy and pursued only by a few hobbyists. It would have been easy for the federal government to discourage personal computers generally and word processing in particular. That action would have saved the economies of entire communities in the Northeast. It would have been the smart decision, but only for a generation. Then America would have been left with a lower level of technology that no one else in the world wanted.

How much of our present wealth would have gone elsewhere? That is a rhetorical question because we would have lagged in virtually every area of our economy. Welcome to the third world. Our biggest industries would now involve stripping our natural resources to supply raw materials to the leading economies, much the condition to which the old Soviet Union has been reduced. America has been a leader not because the government has managed its economy. It has been a leader because the free market is the best determinant of success.

There is a role for the government in a free market economy. We must have some regulations, for example. And we should tout the tremendous scientific advances that have come about through research sponsored by the Department of Defense, NASA, and other agencies. Since WWII these agencies have funneled money into projects that have spurred American technology and made us a powerhouse. This is a legitimate role for government. Imagine what a spur to the flanks of the staggering economy would have occurred in 2008 and 2009 if only a fraction of the money given to those amassing capital had been given in grants and contracts to develop additional technology or expanding the space program. Developing technology that is not feasible for private firms to develop because there either is no immediate payback or the payback appears too long term, or the amounts of money needed are too immense, has been a wonderful blessing. Yet the complex has accepted this role largely in response to the external threats or challenges. Since the fall of the Soviet Union, the research and development has fallen dramatically. We are still using forty year old technology to shuttle astronauts to and from space. The military does not even bother with umbrella programs that would have stimulated entire new areas of development.

Let us look briefly at the tumble of the economy in 2008. It had been the policy of the federal government to encourage home ownership. It had done so by guaranteeing certain mortgages when the house-buyer otherwise would not have been able to obtain the loan. These buyers would not have received loans, or at least loans on such favorable terms, using customary and traditional criteria because their financial positions were not strong enough. But with the guarantees of the federal government, these people could obtain loans. The goal of these programs was noble and for years they offered many people the opportunity to acquire homes. But by 2008 these programs had been corrupted. Politicians had insisted they make loans to people who had no reasonable chance of re-paying the loan unless they could win big in a lottery. This fueled an unnatural rise in housing prices. Not surprisingly, the number of foreclosures began to skyrocket.

Just to keep our terms straight, remember that the buyer gives a mortgage, a secured interest, to a bank on their house in return for the loan. Although we often say that "the bank gave me a mortgage", that is not actually what is happening; it is the other way around. Anyway, while the housing market was going great guns thanks to the liberal lending policies, banks and investment houses were selling a new type of investment vehicle called a mortgage derivative. Up to that time mortgages usually had been sold in huge bundles. When a default in payment occurred, it was relatively easy to go in to the bundle, fish out that particular mortgage, and foreclose on the property. The pension fund or investor who held the bundle of mortgages could always figure out what the bundle was worth. That made the bundle saleable if the investor wanted to sell it before the loans matured.

Then a clever investment house invented the derivative. Let us say I have ten bundles each of one hundred mortgages, with each mortgage worth one dollar. That's one thousand dollars I hold in mortgages. If there is a default, I know exactly which one of my bundles is losing that loan. In fact, I know specifically which house is going into foreclosure, and I can take steps to mitigate the loss by seizing the property and selling it. Moreover, if I want cash, I could sell one of my bundles or even one of the mortgages. But being a clever lad, instead of selling the security, the mortgage, I decide that I am going to sell shares in my thousand mortgages. In fact I am going to sell one thousand shares at a dollar apiece. Those one thousand shares are backed up by my one thousand mortgages. The buyer of a single share owns one-one thousandth of each of the thousand mortgages. The difficulty now is for the buyer of those shares who wants to know the current value of his share. If there is a foreclosure, the share will have lost value, but it may not be easy to calculate exactly when and how much. Unlike the bundles, this share, or derivative, is not tied to discrete mortgages. You would think investors would shy away from these instruments, but in fact they come with a great sales line, "the risk is spread out to a much greater extent than if you had only bought a bundle of mortgages."

Let's make it even better. Say that my pal, Biff, has another thousand mortgages, and he does the same thing I did: he decides to sell a thousand shares at a dollar apiece. But instead of Biff and I doing it separately, we form a new company into which we each put our thousand shares. The total value in the new company is thus two thousand dollars, all backed by mortgages. Sounds great. This new company will sell shares, but we decide to have it sell four thousand shares at fifty cents instead of two thousand at one dollar each so that the shares are more affordable. By now, each share has no direct relation to any particular mortgage; it is at least twice removed. But the good news is that the risk is even more spread out, and it's an even better sales line. The bad news is that we know foreclosures are happening, we just don't know what they are doing to the value of our particular derivatives. Worse news is that the number of these foreclosures is skyrocketing. Still worse is that the housing prices are tumbling to levels that may be even less than the amount of the loans. Suddenly we do not know if the mortgage loans are sufficiently collateralized. There is no reasonable way I can estimate how the value of the derivative is affected by the foreclosures in Detroit or the falling home prices in Nevada because I cannot tell if my share is ultimately backed by those mortgages.

Eventually it could get all sorted out, but as the derivatives combine and re-combine, it becomes practically impossible for an investor to know what his investment is worth. In the failing housing market of 2008, with rising foreclosures and falling prices, no one knew the value of the hundreds of billions of dollars of these derivatives. Although the derivatives were theoretically backed by mortgages; from a practical standpoint, no mortgage could be traced to any particular derivative, and even if you could, you would probably find that the loan was under-collateralized. Because no one wanted to buy something where the value was unclear, the accounting rules required that the derivative be listed as zero value. Derivatives had become "toxic". This was bad news for the investors and investment houses.

Fortunately we live in a free market and the free market can automatically correct these events. The government programs that had encouraged bad lending practices were admonished because no one in the future would buy their mortgage backed investments unless they changed their ways; and the banks, investors, and investment houses learned that the derivatives were a bad idea because they lost hundreds of billions of dollars, and in some instances failed. What a fairy tale ending.

Fairy tale, indeed. The free market was not allowed to correct itself. The government complex stepped in and made a terrible situation worse. First of all it took hundreds of billions of dollars from taxpayers and bought up all of the toxic assets. This alone was a staggering betrayal of Americans by their own government. Unsound investments were rewarded and free market losers were turned into government complex winners. The cherry on this particular sundae was that the federal complex developed a program so that the mortgage-backed loans had to be written down to accommodate the bad lending practices. This is the government telling banks that if they lend ten dollars, they might have to be satisfied with only eight or nine dollars coming back. This is simply untenable for a bank and the lesson is that the bank should not do mortgages unless the government will stay involved; unless the banks can be dependent on the complex. This is a bonus for the federal complex because it leaves the complex indefinitely in a position of control. The sin of the complex was less in giving away the common man's money to the wealthy, but more in the gutting of the free market.

The inescapable question is why a government would do such things. Why would a government deliberately create chaos in a system that has afforded so much to so many? Particularly in an area like mortgages which are the fuel for the building industry, and where the law and investment vehicles have evolved over hundreds of years.

The answer is that the federal complex moves to create reliance on the complex. Always. The reliance created in this debacle is the reliance of banks and financial houses who now know that if they are big enough, the complex will back their losses. Then there is the reliance by the investor who knows that if he or she buys a bad investment from the right investment house, the government will have the common man guarantee the return. There is also the likelihood that for banks to write mortgages henceforth, some ongoing involvement by the complex will be required. The complex does not care if there are winners or losers in the market. It does not care if the budget is balanced. It cares only about extending its control over the economy and our lives. The best way to do that is for the complex to destroy the viability of the free market. The bigger the mess that the federal complex can make, the more likely that the complex will be required to stay involved and control that sector of the economy, if not directly, then through dependence. The complex always moves to create reliance on itself.

Undeniably, the federal complex's central management could work well for a time. Its activities could stabilize an otherwise volatile market situation by saving jobs. They would keep people employed and help the politicos get elected. Heavens knows the entire state of Michigan should have gotten on their hands and knees in gratitude to either the Almighty or the UAW when General Motors was bailed out. But in the long run bailouts hurt America. They hurt our competitiveness because they undercut the free market. If banks do not work, they should fail. If investment houses create investment devices that are malarkey, they should fail. Putting the taxpayer in a position where he or she underwrites the losses or guarantees the investment is not fair. It taxes the taxpayer twice: once with the initial hit and then again with the loss of American competitiveness.

Power corrupts money. The control of the federal complex is growing. It corrupts the free market. The complex creates chaos and then forces a reliance on itself to escape the chaos. The federal complex creates this pattern time and again because it enables the complex to expand its control. This control will take a vibrant economy and change it into a managed bureaucratic mish-mash. For a while this mish-mash will look more comfortable, and be a lot easier on the pocketbook and the ulcers until the breakdowns begin. And this brings us closer to a time when the American economy ceases to be free market driven. Instead we become a nation where the economy is the handmaiden of the government complex: neat, controlled, and, for the short term, stable. We become a socialist nation with a managed economy. The federal government complex begins to control every aspect of our lives.

Many will argue that the loss of the free market is no great loss at all. They point out that the free market is not being lost; it is just being modified. Some of its fangs are pulled to ease the hurt on the losers. Then we will look for partners with economies that are also losing their teeth, probably Western Europe, and we will draw closer to them. In the meantime India or China will unleash the free market, make real the Promise and the Hope, and slip loose the power of the common man. Then we will sink to a lower status and our children's children will look to emigrate to Asia for opportunity. With the intervention of the federal complex it becomes difficult if not impossible to distinguish the winners from the losers. One could point out that the federal complex has not just blurred the difference, but has transformed the losers into the winners.

But is this really what happens when we lose the free market? Why insist that our liberty is tied to a free market? Can we not have the pleasant vibes of a managed or controlled economy and still keep chugging along with no one left behind? We are fortunate to be living in the twenty-first century and can look back at the track record of managed economies. We can see their results. Let us turn to them now.

CHAPTER EIGHT

Managed Economies

The federal complex moves America towards a managed economy, the ultimate expansion of power. For Americans this should be a line we will not cross. The reason is that we can look at what has happened in the last century to countries that have chosen to have managed economies or have had managed economies forced upon them. In the next several pages we will look at controlled economies in general and Russia's in particular. Prior to its collapse, the Union of Soviet Socialist Republics had the world's oldest managed economy, and in its rise and fall there are several lessons if we care to learn them. We will see that managed economies are inconsistent with our understanding of the rights of the common man to life, liberty, and the pursuit of happiness.

Another phrase for "managed economy" is "socialist economy" and it has been the system of all communist countries.

In fact the history of communism is the history of managed economies on our planet. Karl Marx and Frederic Engels invented the theoretical underpinnings for this political and economic system in the mid-nineteenth century. Although socialist parties and writings had been around for decades, until Marx they primarily relied for justification on the moral weight of correcting the terrible conditions and exploitation that occurred in the industrial revolution. Naked capitalism had given the few unparalleled wealth, but at the cost of living conditions near or below slavery for many. Marx and Engels took the socialist ideal and lifted it to an analytical social science. In their view not only was communism just, it was inevitable, and they believed that they could prove it scientifically. They expected that the world would evolve into a communist system just as surely as they believed that Darwin had just shown that men had evolved from apes. Communism was coming, and the only question was where it would begin.

What would drive the world into socialism, into a worker's paradise, were the inherent inequities created by the industrial revolution: the immense amount of wealth generated coupled with the appalling distribution of that wealth. That distribution, or lack of it, had created profound and widespread misery. Because the industrial revolution created the conditions, those countries where the industrial revolution was most advanced would lead the way into socialism. It was in the factories where the misery was greatest and where the workers reached the critical mass necessary to ignite the wildfire of socialist revolution.

According to doctrine, communism would not and could not develop in an agrarian society because farmers could not reach the level of political maturity needed to bring about the communist revolution. Communist doctrine was clear: this wildfire could not start with the rural peasants. Almost by definition they were not part of the industrial revolution. By their very occupation they were spread out over the countryside, and by their nature they were largely illiterate mugs who dreamt only of a few square yards of land that they could call their own. In the Russia of 1917 the peasants were the vast majority of the population. And they were not just largely illiterate, they were completely illiterate and had been beaten low for a thousand years, pushed face down so long that they could not tell which way was up: poor material for a socialist revolution. So, because there was so little industrial development when compared with the rest of Western Europe and the United States, the last place in Europe that was considered fertile ground for socialism was Russia. The violent revolution, and that is what was expected, would occur in the most industrialized countries first and then spread. In the late nineteenth century and the first decade of the twentieth the most likely candidates were Germany and England, followed closely by the United States and France. In those countries capitalism was strongest; ergo, those countries would become communist first. The race was on. And on. And on. Nothing happened. There was a commune set up in Paris that failed, some rioting here and there, a big happy communist party in Germany, a few revolts, but no revolution anywhere.

Communism did not catch on when and where it should have. One reason was probably the rise and development of a propertied middle class: shopkeepers, small manufactories, practitioners of professional services and skilled trades. The Bourgeoisie. The Bourgeoisie is that class of people who, in a nutshell, are doing well enough and hope to do better. They are not angry or upset. They might be envious of the rich and famous, but who knew, next year they might be rich and famous themselves. There were many things they still wanted like a better car or a bigger house, but the last thing they wanted was a revolution. In a revolution they could lose whatever they had. Someone would burn it to the ground out of spite, or take it by force and redistribute it to the miserable masses, to the "Dark People" as they were called in tsarist Russia. No revolution for the Bourgeoisie, thank you very much. The Bourgeoisie would talk to you about reform and justice and equity. They loved to talk about old traditional values, but they did not want to talk about revolution. So there may have been a lot of miserable poor people exploited in factories and mines, but there were enough members of the Bourgeoisie to make the political and economic system stable enough, and their numbers were growing.

By 1914 even Lenin had given up on any communist revolution occurring in Europe and particularly in Russia. He wrote that he did not expect to live to see it. For decades he had lived a nomadic existence in Western Europe and at the outbreak of war he moved to Switzerland with his wife. To see Lenin was to see an unremarkable man: medium tall, balding in middle age, slightly paunched and stooped over. He liked reading in libraries, hiking in the mountains with his wife, and earned a living by writing articles and living on money from donations. When he was younger, he had done a year or two in Siberia in semi-comfortable exile which established his revolutionary credentials. He spent most of his energies in bitter ranklings with other exiled Russian communists over doctrinal issues such as whether the top communist steering committee should be self-appointed die-hards who willed themselves to power (Bolsheviks) or should be selected by vote of the broader membership (Mensheviks). Except for a few thousand faithful souls no one cared because there was no revolution nor could anyone see one coming. Lenin was, of course, of the Bolshevik persuasion and to all appearances naught but a pettifogging ideologue who would do better if he would just get a nice steady job stamping library books somewhere.

But that is judging the book by its cover although it probably would have been a safe judgment if WWI had not happened. But the war did happen and in March 1917, almost three years into the conflict, the Tsar did the unthinkable: he abdicated. Until that moment Tsar Nicholas had been an absolute and autocratic despot, ruling by divine right. What a saga that debacle is. Nothing is left out: a feckless autocrat ruling a country still in the Middle Ages, the heir apparent with an incurable disease, a whirling glittering society set amidst white snows and surrounded by shadowy forests where wolves howl mournfully like a Greek chorus, and all the while a dark debauched priest whispers in the ear of a beautiful half-mad tsarina. And at the end everybody dies. What's not to love? Wagner could not have written such a Gotterdammerung.

Anyway, at the time the war began in 1914, almost all Russians were Dark People: nameless faceless peasants, more like beasts of burden than men or women, who lived short hard lives void of grace or liberty. The gross domestic product on a per capita basis was only about one-third that of the West. To contemporary Americans Russia was nightmarish, and it was difficult for them to imagine how they could be on the Tsar's side in a war.

After the Tsar's abdication in March 1917 there simply was no government. There was the Duma, a powerless embryonic legislature that had been doing nothing but whining for a few years. It had existed at the sufferance of the Tsar as an outlet for some of the anger and misery. Whenever the Tsar tired of the speeches and the tsar-bashing, he simply would tell the members to go home.

The Duma did not cause the Tsar to abdicate. He managed to mess things up badly enough without their help. The Duma just happened to be there at the same time. After the abdication the Duma was no more in control of Russia than a baby strapped onto the back of a wild horse is in control. But in 1917, given time and an ounce of nurturing, the Duma might have matured and mastered that wild horse. It could have become a parliament, a congress that could have been a new life for Russia. It came so close that it was heartbreaking, but in Russia democracy was murdered in its infancy. And the murderer was none other than one of the most remarkable men of the twentieth century: the hitherto pettifogger, Lenin.

To grasp the magnitude of the murder, understand that true communism is democratic. It can be argued that it is more democratic even than a democracy. The heart of that communist democracy is the soviet. A soviet is founded on any identifiable community of interest such as a factory. The workers in the factory all get together and form a soviet. It is more than a union. A union only has existence in opposition to management who represent the owners. If there is a soviet there is no management because there are no identifiable owners; the state owns or controls everything. The soviet directs the factory: it is all of the workers getting together and voting. They meet and vote on conditions, policies, production levels, and relations with other soviets. This is direct democracy. And it is constant; a soviet is democracy in perpetual motion. They meet as often as they want, and vote as often as they want about anything and everything. Each worker is a member of the soviet and has a voice. They may even have their own police force controlled directly by the soviet. It is akin to the true democracies of the old Greek city states except that the boundary of the soviet is more of a community of interest rather than geography. Truly, what could be more fun, more democratic? The soviet might elect representatives to meet with representatives of other soviets in workers' councils, a kind of soviet of soviets. It was recognized that leaders would emerge, but these leaders would be the products of the soviets. All political and economic power rested squarely with the people in their soviets.

The political and economic power in Marxist communism is strictly from the bottom up. Each individual worker gets a vote in the soviet. Because the soviet does not rely on geography, it does not need national boundaries to protect its interests. In fact national boundaries inhibit and limit its ability to function. A worker's loyalties are thus not to a national government, but to the soviet and to a socialist system that perpetuates the soviets and which recognizes no national boundaries.

Even soldiers can form soviets. In March 1917 there were about 160,000 soldiers in and around Petrograd which is what they were calling St. Petersburg soon after the war started because the "burg" sounded unpatriotically German. Petrograd was the seat of power, the heart of tsarist Russia. Agents of the socialist parties had worked their way through these regiments like termites through an old house. What probably precipitated the Tsar's resignation was the fact that the regiments began forming soviets or proto-soviets to discuss the political situation. They refused to quell the civil disturbances. To top it off, they also decided to shoot most of their officers. So any identifiable group can form a soviet, and the essence of the soviet is raw unbridled democracy.

At the time of the Tsar's resignation, the Duma was composed largely of elected representatives and truly represented the political spectrum from adamant monarchists to diehard communists. However, from Lenin's communist perspective the Duma was a continuation of the capitalist system because the ownership or control of the factories remained where it always had been: with the capitalists. While the Duma bumbled along to disaster, the communists were busy setting up or expanding soviets in the factories and in the various regiments. In reality during March 1917 there were two democratic systems, the Duma and the soviets. At times the two even worked together and most of the communists, at times even including the Bolsheviks, saw their future as lying inside the Duma.

That changed in April 1917 with the arrival of Lenin. Lenin electrified the Bolsheviks. He saw the correct path to power for the Bolsheviks, and he had the unbending will and clear judgment to stay on that path. His announced "April Theses" insisted that the workers be armed, that Russia immediately sue for peace, and, most importantly for our discussion, that all means of production be nationalized, owned or controlled by the state. He knew that this was impossible to attain in the Duma, so he refused to cooperate or work inside that body. He knew that if he allowed the Bolsheviks to work inside the Duma's political system, they would have to compromise. The Bolsheviks would then be no more than one more party on the political spectrum. This he refused to do; he declined to take half a loaf.

Lenin had seen communism march along in other countries as one of a multitude of political parties. In not one of those countries had the communists come to power, and, even worse, the communists had to so compromise themselves to get along with others that in the end, Lenin despised them. When Lenin had lived in Switzerland, he had found the Swiss branch of the party so compromised that he would not even be civil when its leader came to call. True communism is an extreme, and like all extremes does not play well with others. Lenin knew that communism could not attain power by playing inside the political system; it would only lose its steam. So, he refused to work inside the Duma, the provisional government. He demanded that the Bolsheviks alone build and control the soviets. He had no use for the Mensheviks, those communists who were generally willing to work within the Duma.

Lenin's political acumen was not his only gift. He also could persuade people that he was right, not just the other intellectuals and the exiles who returned to Russia, but the semi-literate factory workers and soldiers. While it is not always easy now to see the man, one point on which all of his contemporaries agree is that Lenin had the gift of breaking down complex ideas into digestible mouthfuls that could be understood by everyone, and his logic would appear irrefutable. Slowly, and with many reverses, he exposed the Duma as an empty box that blew away in November of that year. Granted, the box was empty because he had helped empty it, but Bolshevik socialism had triumphed.

Sort of. They controlled Petrograd and a few urban centers like Moscow, but outside of these centers there was nothing- a void. In fact it was worse than a void because there were competing ideologies and they were armed to the teeth. Lenin, with his chill vision, had expected civil war, and with his even colder will, welcomed the violence as a sign of ascendancy.

Lenin took control of the cities and seized the means of production. All factories were owned and operated by the State. For the first time since whenever, the industrial economy of a country was centrally controlled. It was a disaster. With the ravages of WWI, the dislocations of the civil war, the misallocations caused by the Bolsheviks own mismanagement, and the total stifling of enterprise, the Russian economy did not recover. It remained a basket case for decades, a misshapen stunted homunculus that gave birth to generations of death and misery.

In 1928, fully ten years after the implementation of a planned economy, Russia still had not reached the level of industrial output that it had attained in pre-war 1913. Worse was yet to come. The socialist historians tend to blame the poor economic recovery on the depredations of the West, and while there is some truth to that, the whole truth is that every major power engaged in that war did recover, even Germany, and went on to greater prosperity except for Russia.

In 1917 the Bolsheviks saw themselves surrounded by enemies, both internally and externally, and they were probably right. The bulwark of communism- the democracy of the soviets- was the first casualty of the revolution. There was a strict party line and deviation was caught by the secret police, an organization that grew more pervasive, efficient, and deadly than anything the tsars had unleashed. The shell of the soviets lived on, but democracy died quickly and unmourned.

Russia became a dictatorship by committee, and the committee was chaired by Lenin. For years Russia either was in a state of civil war or on the brink of civil war. The soviets, which had hitherto been comprised of socialists of all stripes ceased to function in a meaningful way. Democracy was an egg that Lenin broke to make his omelet. Aggravating the situation in 1917 was the added stress that neither Lenin nor the other leaders imagined that Russia would have to go it alone. They viewed Russia as an anomaly; the revolution had occurred there out of sequence. It meant that the revolutions in Germany and England were already late and could be expected momentarily. In fact, Lenin and Trotsky publicly expressed serious doubts as to whether the revolution in Russia could even survive without the international revolution. But they had underestimated their secret police. If Lenin would not give Russians a communist democracy, he would at least put them under the thumb of a first rate killing machine: the Chekha.

So, Lenin and Trotsky waited for the international revolution. And they waited. By the early 1920's it was beginning to sink in that Russia was alone. This further increased the Bolshevik's fears of isolation and led them to deemphasize the international aspects of communism in favor of the narrower interests of Russia. Their desire to control every aspect tightened.

Then Lenin died suddenly in 1924. Eventually the chairman's hat fell to Stalin which was a surprise to everyone because Trotsky had been the favored son. A surprise to everyone, that is except Stalin. Stalin was not good at juggling the theoretical aspects of communism, but he was as an excellent street fighter, a real sociopathic brute. He was the right man for the job ahead. Meaningful power had already ceased to reside with the Soviets, and Stalin finished off even the pretense by declaring that voting would be nationwide, and not by soviets. While Russia was a socialist state, it had ceased in any meaningful way to be a Marxist state. Russia had become a socialist autocracy.

Stalin inherited an economy that was a disaster. The industrial output of Soviet Russia did not equal what had been under the Tsar and could not compare with the West. Nothing, certainly no amount of slogans and propaganda, could correct the fact of the appalling state of industry. The living conditions of the urban worker were tragic and reflected the desperate poverty of the country. It is difficult to believe that the population of any western country would have considered them acceptable. Then in the late 1920's the worst that could happen, happened. Not only was the output of the urban industries abysmal, but the industries were unable or unwilling to make manufactured goods that the people in the country wanted. The peasants, who were always one harvest away from starvation themselves, were unwilling to trade their foodstuffs with the cities: the cities produced nothing that the farmers wanted. This portended a disaster for Russian communism in general and for Stalin in particular. Stalin ordered the Russian armies to go into the countryside to seize the food, grain and animals. This worked until the peasants began burning their grain and killing their animals rather than letting them fall into the hands of the commissars.

This was sheer disaster. Stalin had to make a choice. He could either allow communism to collapse and himself along with it, or he could make war on the peasants. He made war on the peasants. He forced the peasants off their individual plots of ground and into collective farms. The peasants were bitterly unhappy at this and refused. Over the next few years Stalin ended resistance by killing and starving tens of millions of peasants. Voila, collective farms.

Throughout the ensuing seventy odd years of its existence, the old Soviet Union was unable to compete economically with the West. When the Soviet Union finally gave up the ghost in 1989, the gross domestic product was only a little over half that of the United States, and on a per capita basis was barely forty percent of that for an American. The toll in human misery was immeasurable. Even as late as the early 1950's over fifteen percent of the gross domestic product may have come from the gulag prison camps across the country. For the federal complex to move our economy towards a managed system knowing the horrors that await is unconscionable.

What the twentieth century has shown is that communism inevitably becomes a dictatorship. We know that from the Russian experience, and that of China, Cuba, and a host of lesser lights including the psychotic vaudevillians in North Korea. Lenin's Bolshevik path is the only successful route for communism. It takes an individual of unwavering determination to bring the communist party to power, and once in power, the pressures to maintain that power result in a dictatorship. Democracy is the last thing that can be tolerated, regardless of the formal party line. Which brings us to a comparison with fascism. The only real difference between the two is who controls the means of production. If the state owns or controls them, then the dictatorship is communist and the economy is managed by the State. If the means of production are still privately owned, then the dictatorship is fascist. In fairness, communist dictators are generally lower key, less likely to be interested in personal gain and the trappings of power. At the risk of delving into psychology, if the person who became the communist dictator was motivated by personal gain, being a communist organizer would probably have been a poor career choice in the first place.

A communist or fascist leader does not come to power on his own. There are a tremendous number of associates, underlings, and true believers for whom the leader embodies the principles that brought him to power in the first place. They would put the leader under tremendous personal pressure to assume a chairmanship, presidency, or chancellorship for life. "Who else has the unerring judgment to guide us?"

A fascist regime usually does not survive the death of its leader whereas a communist regime usually does. There are a host of reasons for this, but the basic reason is that a communist regime has seized the means of production. When Marx and Engels used the term "means of production" they were mainly thinking of factories, mines, and any other economic endeavors which were inherently exploitative. Now the term would also include banks, oilfields, computer and system companies, or any entity that generates or controls wealth. Exploitation of workers may have little to do with the generation of that wealth. When a communist regime comes to power, the first thing it does, or at least is supposed to do, is seize these privately held means of production. This is never, or at least rarely, done peacefully. This is because the previous owners of the privately held means of production were the capitalists who were the bugbears and trolls of communist ideology, and, needless to say, unhappy at the prospect of losing their property. These capitalists would be exiled or "re-educated" if they were lucky. If they were not lucky then, in that wonderful Trotskyism, they would be "liquidated". If the seized enterprise was owned by a corporate entity that had no recognizable owner, or might even be owned by some foreign entity, the seizure might be bloodless, but in any event it was permanent. This massive change digs up the roots of national life, shakes the old soil from them, and then replants them in the totally foreign pot of state control. Virtually every aspect of a citizen's life changes when the communists take power. The economy is directed.

The state could not easily change from communist to non-communist even if it wanted to. Everyone's jobs, livelihood, and mode of living would be tied to maintaining the new status quo. To change it would require another revolution. The easiest route is for the communist leadership to come together and select another leader, any leader. The revolutionary spirit may have founded the communist party in a particular nation, but it is the very opposite, the lack of revolutionary spirit that enables the regime to continue.

The fascist regime has an easier if shorter life. It has not up-ended the economy and changed the system of ownership, so switching from democracy to fascism or vice-versa is not the total shake that occurs with a change to communism. In the West, at least in America, we tend to think of fascists as monsters and communists more as misguided, if godless, altruists. Yet the monstrousness of the fascists is short-lived. The archetypes of fascist regimes in the twentieth century were Germany and Italy, but in neither country did the regime outlast the death of its leader. In fact the changeover to democracy in both countries came about with surprising ease, particularly because neither country had any real history of strong democratic traditions. Even Japan, a militaristic monarchy since history began, made a seemingly effortless switch to a generally free market democracy in a few years.

The antithesis of communism is not democracy. In fact, Marxist communism is more democratic in theory than any extant democracy including that of the United States or England. Remember the soviets. The antithesis of communism is the free market; it is state ownership and state control versus private ownership and private control.

Free market capitalism requires the acknowledgement of human rights if it is to function properly. Goods, services, money, and, most importantly, ideas must be able to flow unimpeded if society is to obtain the benefits of the free market. There are times when it appears as though the free market is compatible not only with democracy, but also with fascism, dictatorships, monarchies, oligarchies, and any other form of governance that leaves the means of production in private hands.

For example, the European fascists in the first half of the twentieth century largely left their respective economies in private hands. Although those regimes allied themselves with moneyed interests, and those interests with the regimes, the factories, resources, and land still remained largely in private hands.

The issue though is not how an economy looks from the outside; even the greased and smoothly running communist system can look great for a while. The issue is whether everything is flowing within. Does the society restrict women to making babies and pulling a plow if the horse dies? If so, then the economy has lost one half of its potential brainpower. Imagine that economy in competition with an economy that has double the brainpower. Does the society restrict people with bushy hair to street maintenance and repair, or prohibit people over six feet from going to college. The restrictions sound silly, don't they? But it is not just that the restrictions cull out potentially productive people, but the mere fact that a society is willing to accept such restrictions and limitations, such negations of the human rights of individuals, that neither the economy nor the society can be open and dynamic.

But let us now turn the restrictions around. If your father is a party member in good standing, the government will pay for your college. If you make cars for a favored company that goes bankrupt, the government will buy the company and guarantee your job. If you are a member of a splintered voting group and do not do well on a job test, the government will either discard the test or change the scoring. These moves restrict the economy and consequently restrict human rights no less than restricting bushy haired persons to only street maintenance and repair. Einstein, with his unruly mop, was a wonderful physicist, but probably would be lousy spreading asphalt. However in a free market that honors human rights, if Einstein had wanted to spread asphalt, he could have spread it. To have forced him to be a physicist would have been as intolerable as forcing him not to.

Restricting human rights puts kinks into the free market. The market can still function up to a point, but it has to work around these kinks. The economy and the society pay a price for these kinks in terms of human dignity in the society and productivity in the economy. That is why a free market does not play well with fascists, oligarchs, or dictators. It does not play well when money is siphoned off for protection or bribes. Siphoning money puts kinks in the economy. Any economy with kinks will be out-produced by the economy without the kinks or with the fewest kinks. They discourage people from doing well.

A society with these kinks will always experience an out-migration of its people. Americans are not flocking to live in Islamic countries, nor was the Berlin wall built to keep the West from immigrating to East Germany. A society cannot function well if it accepts these kinks any more than an economy can do well. It is like living with a ball and chain around your leg. You may be able to get by, but you will not do well with such an impediment. You will always be outperformed by a similar person without the ball and chain. The person who has such an impediment may finally decide that it is natural and best to have such a ball and chain, and believes that everyone should have one. Furthermore, if others do not share that belief, then they are infidels unworthy of life. Or that person may decide to go to a country without the balls and chains.

The difficulty with the fascist or monarchical regimes, at least economically, is that they try to freeze the economy, make it function as it has always functioned. They can make little charts and diagrams of how it all works. If you have money when a fascist regime takes over and support the regime financially and politically, then you have a good chance of garnering more money and a small chance that this regime will seize what you have. The dictator or king wants to deal with the same supportive people. By their nature they do not want new ideas or new people that will upset their plans. So, for a while the economy seems to function and look great, but it will not be able to compete over the long term.

Certainly there have been times when a fascist or socialist economy looks as though it is on the cutting edge. For example, the Soviet Union was able to put a rocket into space before America, Nazi Germany had advanced weaponry, and in the late nineteenth century Japan transformed its military from feudal to modern in a single generation. A managed economy and its society can force resources into certain channels much more quickly than a free economy. If the goal is to get modern warships, the fascist or communist state can do so quickly and rearrange resources by fiat. It can most quickly get the best performance by marshaling existing technology. However the system fails over the long haul. Such a state can re-order the existing technology, or stretch the existing technology, or acquire the technology to accomplish great things today. What it cannot do is to let that technology evolve with new ideas generation after generation. In fact it will not do it at all unless spurred by the accomplishments of a competing free market system.

There has never been a Marxist communist nation. There have been Leninist communist nations in which a person or a small group of persons seize power under the banner of socialism/communism, but every one of those countries is a socialist dictatorship. For decades while in exile before 1917 Lenin tore holes in the communist movement by insisting that communist leadership not come from the elected representatives of the soviets, but from a handful of individuals who willed themselves to power and a chairman who embodied the revolution. There is another word for that form of government:

"dictatorship". This does not make the proclaiming of communism by the peoples of these countries an empty gesture. Nominal adherence to the communist ideology provides the glue that holds the regime and the populace together. That and a good secret police service. Furthermore, the communist doctrine itself became a mechanism for holding and binding other countries, other dictatorships, which would then nominally adhere to a similar doctrine. This was a great way for a dictator in some third world country to stay in power. Instead of being a sleazy warlord, he could proclaim himself a Leninist communist, seize every asset in the country and divide it among his followers, and never have to resign. This was a particularly popular ploy in sub-Saharan Africa where it was used to systematically strip wealth from generations of the populace. Following WWII America also set up a number of puppet dictators, but it was always clumsy when the dictator kept winning elections every time for decades and their opponents were sent to prison or executed. It is too easy to see through a sham democracy. However when a dictator spouts communist catchphrases, it even gives him an aura of legitimacy, a certain cachet. When he enslaves the population and kills his opposition he gets to say he is doing it for "the people". It is so much more respectable, more politically-correct.

The importance of this outward adherence to Leninist communism also provides the leadership with the solution to a sticky problem: the orderly transfer of power following the death of the founding dictator. It avoids civil war which no one in power ever wants. The layer of politicos below that of the founding dictator agree on who is to succeed without killing one another. This can be tricky because if there are serious factions in this layer, there is a distinct possibility that the winning faction will kill the losing faction and their families to boot. So, if there is some basis for agreement, it can make life easier and safer. Any basis will work, such as being the son of the prior dictator who has been groomed for this transition. This happens in North Korea, where the toadish family who rules that country must be an embarrassment to good communists everywhere, but they can at least get power passed without a civil war.

Communist leaders are the same as dictators and, realistically, cannot voluntarily resign. The terms of their leadership never come to an end. However, remember that they are virtually mandated to stay in office because of the underlying doctrine of Leninist communism which says that only they embody the true ideals of the revolution. So, in addition to the personal danger if they should leave office, there is the doctrinal justification for remaining.

As an aside I cannot help but compare these fascist and socialist dictators with our own George Washington. Washington's voluntary relinquishment of power is absolutely astounding and unparalleled in recorded history. Of all of the gifts possessed by this extraordinary man, perhaps his finest was being able to rise even above his own genius. Certain pundits point out with much lip-smacking satisfaction that Washington was not perfect. However, we already knew this. As far as I know only one man has ever been perfect, and even he relied on his Father.

The managed economy cannot compete in the long run against a free market economy. Why then do so many countries flirt with a communist or socialist system? When there can be so much more wealth for so many more people in a free market, how in good conscience can leaders want to go down the socialist path? I have to ask the question still one more way for good measure. When there has not been a single managed economy in the history of mankind that has not produced misery, autocracy, and system-wide failure, and there is not a free market economy that does not produce success and democracy, how can people again and again want to move towards a managed economy?

However wonderful communism may sound with all the voting and its promise to empower the common man, in reality it is a disaster. It ends in autocracy. Not once in a while, not sometimes under adverse conditions, not just in response to external threats, but always, every time, and for good. The first casualty is democracy, voting. Soviets simply do not work. Workers setting their own conditions and terms will not work. It will not work because no soviet operates in a vacuum. It is a part and parcel of the fabric of the economy. The miners may only want to work twenty hours each week, but when they do then it ripples out through the rest of the economy. The railway workers may all want every May Day off from their labors, but when they do, the rest of the economy goes out of whack. The miners will dig out the raw ore and the porters will work on May Day, or they will be arrested.

Democracy and human dignity can quickly bring a controlled economy to the point of disaster. Lenin knew it, Stalin knew it, and Mao knew it. However wonderful the democratic soviets sound, they do not work. Their only real usefulness is before the communists come to power. Then they can be the tool that undermines worker discipline, promotes unhappiness, and promises the moon. A soviet is inherently revolutionary if begun in a capitalist economy. It has to be because it promises to assume the role of the owners. It cannot become a true soviet until the capitalist owners have been driven out and the soviet comes into physical control of the factory. Yet in every communist take-over, the soviets, these democratic hearts of the communist theory, become intolerable liabilities.

In a managed economy there must be an overarching bureaucratic and autocratic organization to knit the economy together, an autocratic and bureaucratic organization which sets the output goals so that they can be depended upon, and distributes resources, services, and goods. This has to happen if the economy is to function at all and when it does, it guts the soviets. An economy that is completely socialist must have this top-heavy bureaucratic organization to distribute resources as needed throughout the economy. These cannot be guidelines or a list of hopeful ideas. That is why a managed economy requires an autocracy, and a free market will always be partnered with a democracy. When the federal complex leans us toward a managed or controlled economy, it is guiding us towards an autocracy.

Traditionally we distinguish different economic systems by how raw material, capital, labor, and the finished product are distributed. Socialists distribute them one way and the free market distributes them another way. If we were to look at snapshots of these two, they probably would not look that different: goods and services spitting out at the end of one system and the other. One might compare the snapshots and observe that in the socialist system, the components seem to move more efficiently down pathways that have been smoothed by usage. There is likely to be less friction, fewer spot shortages. Certainly there is none of the wasted effort doing advertising that is present in the free market system. Even if we briefly stress each system, say with a war, and take another snapshot, there is every likelihood that the socialist system responds in a more direct and efficient manner. It immediately readjusts all of its resources by fiat to meet the new threat. Factories can re-tool quickly and redirect their output. If we were to look at the snapshots further, we would probably notice that the socialist economy has full employment. That probably is not true in the free market economy. Then if we looked at the gap between the rich and poor, we would almost certainly notice that there is a smaller gap in the socialist economy than there is in the free market economy. In so many ways the socialist economy, the managed economy, appears more efficient and more equitable.

But if we go beyond the snapshots of the economies and look at the broader society of which the economy is only a factor, we would see that the average standard of living in the free market economy is substantially greater. In an economy where the paths of distribution of the resources and the end products are fixed, there can be few improvements in productivity, no real gains in the standards of living. In fact, both the productivity and the standards of living will move backwards as those smooth paths of distribution develop friction and themselves require greater and greater resources to maintain. We would also see that citizens in the socialist society are trying to emigrate to the free market society. We would see that the socialist society has to rely on secret police and Gestapo tactics to hold their citizenry. And more than that, we would find in the socialist economy that ideas and innovation are stifled. Innovation is a threat in the socialist system because any innovation disrupts the paths of resources or distribution. The commissars have to go back to their superiors, report a disruption, and take some kind of corrective action. Everybody looks bad. It is much easier to arrest the person with the new idea. Such action not only successfully addresses the potential disruption, but it also discourages future potential disruptions.

In a managed economy innovation is a threat to the system. It is disruptive and creates unhappiness. Innovation and change to any existing pathway of resources is discouraged. It is acceptable to innovate while a pathway for resources or distribution is being created, but afterwards innovations become a problem. The managed economy must rely on force to resist innovation. There is no acceptable internal movement for change in a managed economy with one exception, and that is in response to external pressure, usually from a free market economy. A managed economy by its nature is not compatible with human rights. The rights to life, liberty, and the pursuit of happiness cannot exist in a managed economy because human rights inherently give greater dignity to the goals of the individual than to any particular announced goal of the society or economic system. The free market economy bets on the common man. It seeks to protect the dignity of his choices. The managed economy cannot afford that luxury. It cannot afford the potential disruption caused by a common man who is turned loose with his own idea about light bulbs, or internal combustion engines, or computers.

In the snapshot contest for beautiful babies the managed economy is going to get the blue ribbon. But if we take a moving picture, the contest is all over. The free market is going to win every time. Now "every time" sounds like the free market is bragging, and it is. But it is also true. Managed economies have lost every single time in human history. Not ninety percent of the time, not ninety nine percent, but one hundred percent. Game over, or at least it should be over. Managed economies hold back the common man and, consequently, they hold back the standard of living. The common man is reduced to no more value than his economic contribution. He becomes of no more import than the machine he operates. The common man wants to leave a managed economy and will do so if can get to the border. Managed economies have to dehumanize the common man and turn him into a mouse scurrying on the treadmill. It does not matter if the managed economy belongs to a communist, fascist, or monarchical regime; the result is the same.

Historically, there seem to be only two scenarios where managed economies take control. The first is where they replace a society that is essentially feudal in structure. This was the case with Russia and China at the time of their respective revolutions.

It was also true with North Korea. A variant of this is where the societies have not even reached the feudal stage such as sub-Saharan Africa. However, in such backward settings there was never hope for even a Leninist communist system and they collapsed into barbarous autocracies. The second and more familiar scenario in which managed economies have been introduced is at the point of a bayonet. This was the case in Eastern Europe following WWII. But no where ever has a free people voluntarily enslaved themselves to a managed economy.

Managed economies have never tolerated personal freedom. American statesmen occasionally excoriate communist or fascist states for their appalling human rights records. That is like yelling at the neighbor's cat for chasing birds. It is pointless; it is in the nature of cats to chase birds. Managed economies do not have appalling human rights records because they choose to do so. They have appalling human rights records precisely because they are managed economies. They cannot do otherwise.

But there is a scenario where managed economies can triumph. That is to exist in a world where there are no free market economies. If the free market is successfully extinguished here and in the West generally, then there will be nothing that will show the poor performance of the managed economy. The measuring stick will have disappeared and with it any semblance of human rights and dignity. But wiping out every free market economy in the world is an impossible order.

The free market economies of the world cannot be overwhelmed by the less able and less productive socialist economies. But there is another path: persuade these free market economies to commit suicide. That can happen if there is an overarching international body that either obtains agreements from every nation to establish managed economies or has the power to impose such an economy on all nations. If managed economies exist world-wide, then there is no other yardstick against which to measure their poor performance. The threat to America's economy is not that it will be overwhelmed by exterior forces. The much more real threat is that the federal complex will persuade it to commit suicide, to cede power to itself or an international entity.

But if one examines the performance of these managed economies, the results are so poor, and the lifestyle afforded to the citizens so appalling, that is hard to imagine any nation voluntarily choosing such an economic model. Yet people have taken up arms to implement a managed economy again and again, and even here in America there are groups who are eager to adopt such a model. Usually this is done sincerely in the belief that only a managed economy can distribute wealth fairly, correct real and imagined social wrongs, and generally usher in true equality among peoples and nations. The simple fact that managed economies have never done that, but have brutalized and murdered their own populations, and will reduce everyone except the elites to desperate and inescapable poverty makes no difference. It makes no difference to the federal complex because the complex seeks only one thing: more control. Although it should make a difference to the splinter groups who look to the complex for protection, in fact it does not because they accept at face value the simple slogans and pictures that the complex assures them will usher in a new and better era.

A communist state is a socialist state: all means of production are owned or controlled by the state. However, the communists go further in terms of property ownership than the socialists do by abolishing the concept of private property altogether. So all communists are socialists, but not all socialists are communists. Socialist states in general and communist states in particular are not able to compete with free market economies and states. Within a generation the managed economy will have to close its borders both to hold in its population and to bar ideas and ideals generated in the free economies. This is not just usually the case with managed economies; it is the case in one hundred percent of the managed economies. Yet, in America the federal complex persists in moving us in that direction.

A socialist economy must be directed because the state has gutted the free market forces which would determine the distribution of resources and the distribution of production. In a free market the pressure of dollars determines where resources are used. But in a controlled economy the government makes those decisions. Whether in a free market system or a communist system, labor is a resource. In a free market system, segments of the economy bid on labor. An individual can accept the bid or reject the bid and go elsewhere to work. Or he or she can go to school, move to another state and start their own business, or go fishing. But the essence of the free market is that the resources, the capital, the labor, and the finished products have to be able to move freely inside the market. Restricting them causes inefficiencies and waste, although sometimes we have to build in those systemic burrs. For example, an oil company may want to extract oil from the Gulf of Mexico in the cheapest possible manner, but that may put the entire Gulf at risk from a blowout of oil.

In a free market innovations are part of the daily give and take of the market and the market adjusts to account for them. Similarly, human labor has to be free to move. If it is not free, if it is not at liberty to come, to go, to work or not to work, then there is no free market. Slavery, aside from the moral condemnation, is a misallocation that stunts the free market and the economy. When children are forced to work in factories, we have taken the most valuable resource in the economy, the future innovation, and wasted it cruelly.

Americans of certain generations have been frightened by communism. We associate it with the miseries and militarism of the Soviet Union, Red China, Cuba, and others who claim to operate under the communist banner. In reality, these countries are not communist, at least not Marxist communist. Each one of these regimes immediately became a socialist dictatorship: socialist because the state seized and thereafter owned the means of production, and dictatorships because the state's power resided in a single individual or group. This difference between a Marxist state and a socialist dictatorship is not a minor distinction. The former is a communist democracy, which has never existed, and the latter a dictatorship.

We tend to think of socialism in the context of the state providing services for the population at government expense. Services that are commonly thought of in this context are healthcare or welfare. But in fact these services, while commonly found in a socialist/communist system where all of the means of production are owned by the state, are not inherent in socialism or anathema to democracy. Remember that the first social security system originated in a near-absolute monarchy: Germany under the Kaisers. Americans might or might not want their government to ensure healthcare for every American, but the government's doing so does not make America either more or less democratic or more or less socialist. America would become more socialist if the government seized the means of providing those services rather than just paying for them.

This is not just semantics. Many Americans are afraid of the government's paying for a service such as healthcare because it smacks of "socialism" when, in fact, it has nothing to do with socialism. Ensuring that every citizen is provided with healthcare may be "paternalism", or "nanny-statism", or just too expensive, but it is not socialism, nor is there anything inherent in such a policy that puts us onto the path of communism or a managed economy. It would be socialist only if the government also had the means of providing the service. Using charged words such as "socialism" or "leftist" confuses the debate. For example, the VA healthcare system in America is a socialist-type system: the government itself provides the means of production: it owns the hospitals and employs the healthcare personnel. Frankly, in my opinion it is an excellent system, although this may be so to some degree because it is the private system that sets the standard of care.

The important point is that designating a state as socialist does not mean that the state has a paternalistic attitude and provides all of its citizens the essentials of life for free. The state may be too poor to provide anything to anyone, or it may choose not to provide any services. Being socialist only means that it owns or controls the modes of production. A socialist state can adopt a policy of unbridled cruelty towards its own populace such as the Soviet Union did under Lenin and Stalin in the 1920's and 30's, Cambodia did in the 1980's, or North Korea does most everyday. In fact there are many more incentives in a democracy to adopt a paternalistic stance. Politicos can promise free everything to everyone in a democracy and frequently do. To equate socialism with benevolence is a serious mistake that is without any historical evidence.

There may be many reasons why one may choose to be a socialist or a communist, such as wanting all productive capacity owned by the state or desiring that all property be seized and its use redistributed, but to choose it in the belief that socialist means a state kindly disposed to its populace is stupidity or ignorance. If you know someone who is this stupid, you would be doing everyone, and most of all that person, a favor by discouraging them from voting or participating in political processes. The mistaken belief that socialism means free services or human dignity is a confusion that has resulted in the deaths of tens of millions of people and the virtual enslavement of hundreds of millions. I have tried to give a brief history of Russian communism to illustrate that point. I could have used China, North Korea, Eastern Europe, or sub-Saharan Africa.

A controlled economy is a managed economy. When the federal complex designates who masses capital, or the complex forces citizens to underwrite losses sustained by companies, or forces citizens to underwrite risk for companies, or the employees of certain companies are turned into splinter groups, we are becoming a managed economy. This new economy will not be able to compete effectively against free market economies, and the American people also will have lost their liberty. To wait until the process is complete before taking cognizance of the federal complex is to wait until the common man is a pauper and a slave. Whatever you think you can accomplish in the next election is another pipe dream. Both of the major parties are part and parcel of the federal complex.

The states, individually and severally, must stand up for their citizenry. The states created this federal complex, unleashed it, and now serve it. They must say "No"; their citizens will not underwrite corporate losses; their citizens will not guarantee failing securities; and their citizens will not encumber their own liberties by marching down the path to a managed economy. This is not a matter of a state's rights; it is a matter of the state meeting its obligations to defend its citizens. The states did it in 1776 and they have the same obligation now.

CHAPTER NINE

The Free Market

The common man requires a vital free market. Not only does the free market elevate the standard of living of the citizenry, but it is a requirement for liberty. But as there are limits to liberty, such as not hurting one's neighbor, so there must be limits to the free market. Were there no limits then factories would still be able to dump their refuse into the nearest river. Within the lifetime of living Americans rivers have actually caught on fire.

The free market, capitalism, is far too brutal to be unleashed without restraints. It cares nothing for human dignity, for liberty, or the rights of man. It cares only about generating a profit. There are those who will say that in the long term the free market will always correct to incorporate social blessings. For example, at some point people will stop purchasing the products of a company that dumps its refuse in the river; so over time companies will learn not to kill rivers, or oceans, or forests. However, waiting until the river, ocean, or forest is dead encompasses too great a price for us to pay as we wait for the company to learn a lesson. There must be some regulation of the economy to save us from the unbridled effects of capitalism.

Consider the disastrous oil spill in 2010 in the Gulf of Mexico. It may behoove the profits of an oil company to erect and maintain the cheapest possible offshore oil rigs, but when they blow out, then the costs of a major spill and the affects on people's lives are horrendous. There is little incentive to improve oil rigs if the only downside is that someday some people may resist buying the company's products because of the affects on the environment.

There must be some regulatory safeguards, but regulation is not enough because it is not realistic to expect that regulation will cover all permutations of human action. That is why the owners of a company should be held personally liable criminally as well as civilly if there is a failure to reasonably protect the common man. If there were reasonable protections that should have been in place on the oil rig, but the company neglected to employ them or chose not to because of the costs, the owners of the company should be imprisoned for having wantonly destroyed public property.

Similarly, there has been the recent debacle with the mortgage backed securities discussed earlier. Somehow these derivatives met all of the existing regulations, but they still failed. If the derivatives were sold as secured paper, but were not reasonably secured, then again the owners of the companies that sold them should have gone to prison. To pretend that spilling millions gallons of oil into the Gulf of Mexico is just a judgmental mistake like building too many gas stations, or that selling hundreds of billions of dollars in worthless securities is equivalent to an accounting error, is stupid. To arrest, prosecute, and imprison a person for smoking marijuana when major criminals not only walk free, but are financially rewarded, is offensive and intolerable.

Is man the priority, or is money the priority? In the West, and certainly in the view of our nation's Founders, the priority was clear. The dignity belongs to every man, woman, and child; it belongs to the common man. The common man cannot be the servant of the free market. Instead, it is capitalism, the free market, that is to serve the dignity of the common man. Other economic systems reach different conclusions and establish different priorities. In socialist and communist regimes both the common man and the economy serve the state. They must serve the state for the reason we discussed earlier: liberty and a managed economy are anathema to one another.

Unbridled capitalism can unleash appalling greed and inequities such as slavery, child labor, eugenics, and a brutal distribution of wealth. We might as well give each person a gun with the admonition that he can have what he can keep. Far wiser to choose the managed economy and then pray without ceasing.

A man or woman must be able to make the choices inherent in the free market if they are to enjoy liberty, but some choices such as those that reduce the dignity of other men or women are not available. It should not be acceptable for foreign companies that engage in slavery or child labor to be able sell their wares in America, to compete on an equal footing against American companies who do not engage in those practices. The basis for not allowing this practice is not that the foreign company enjoys an unfair competitive advantage. That is a horrible reason because the American company can correct the advantage by going to another country and engaging in similar practices. Even worse, the company could try to engage in them here. No, the basis for rejecting the competition is that the offending company has offended the dignity of the common man by enslaving him and selling the results of that labor.

We touched earlier on the fact that one reason for restraining the free market system is to protect the environment. So much damage has been done so cheaply to the natural world that other than regulation there is not an effective mechanism in the free market to give any reasonable assurance of environmental protection. Fortunately for all of us concern for the environment has become an increasingly important value in

America. Numerous laws and regulations have come into being to restrict economic activity that threatens the environment. Unfortunately the thrust towards minimizing or preventing further damage to the environment has been hijacked and turned into an international swindle.

The scheme is also known as the cap-and-trade laws. The issues encompassed by cap-and-trade have nothing to do with whether America should enact laws to further reduce pollution and protect the environment. The debate now is whether there is global warming and whether that warming is the result of man-made carbon emissions. How one answers those questions has no affect on pollution but neither does cap-and-trade. Cap-and-trade actually excuses the polluters as long as they pay money into a fund which then doles out the money to whoever cries the loudest and most pitifully. And there will be a lot of money. Americans will transfer hundreds of billions of dollars of income into these funds with no appreciable affect on the environment.

Why rational people actually agree to be swindled is beyond the scope of this book. But the fact that money will be moving out of the hands of the common man and into a government rat hole before being redistributed to the wealthy is not beyond the scope. The government complex does not care whether laws make sense nor does it care one whit about pollution. It cares only about control and the transfer of liberty from the common man to itself in the form of power. When the complex transfers money to itself, it transfers power.

The Incredible Shrinking Human Rights

Human rights are the rights enjoyed by every individual person who has existed, exists now, or ever will exist. We are endowed with these rights by God the Creator. This is the foundation of American political philosophy as embodied by the Founders in the Declaration of Independence. What exactly these rights are is arguable, but in America we think of them as life, liberty, and the pursuit of happiness. No God? Then no human rights: no right to life, no right to liberty, no right to pursue happiness. There is a God, you are his creation, and therefore you enjoy a certain dignity simply because you are his creation.

For example, no one has the right to hold you in slavery or to stop you from making the full use of your talents and abilities. Does this mean no one will do those things? Of course not. They may have the power to hold you in slavery, but they do not have the right. In fact you have the right to do whatever you must do to end the slavery and assert your dignity as a human. The idea of human rights, like life, liberty, and the pursuit of happiness, as we understand them has been so ingrained into our consciousness and are so apparent, that we tend to just nod and yawn when we hear them. Most Western countries now subscribe to some form of them either literally or in practice.

However, they make sense only when we acknowledge that they are a gift of a supreme being. If we deny that there is a supreme being, then there is no source, no anchor, for human rights. There is no logical basis then for the Declaration of Independence. Without the Supreme Being serving as a yardstick, we can affirm or deny any human rights using any yardstick that is convenient, pleasant, or politically popular or correct. Rights become self-evident only when we assume the Supreme Being. They are not self-evident without that assumption. The whole idea of human rights sounds simplistic to the American ear today, but the idea of a state founded on the assumption of human rights was revolutionary when Thomas Jefferson put it on paper in the 1770's. It was electrifying. The old European monarchies were never the same. Even today in most of the world such a declaration would land you in prison if not worse. Muslim states do not acknowledge that women have rights equal to a man, or that non-believers have any substantive rights at all. The equal dignity of all humans is heresy in a Muslim state. No country with an autocratic polity views human rights as anything other than treason. And with good reason.

Civil rights, on the other hand, are the rights that the government grants to its citizenry. They are not self-evident and are not given by God. These rights are given because the government has the power to do so. Voting is a civil right. God does not care whether you get to vote or not, and he does not care for whom you vote regardless of the contrary view of many commentators. Voting is a right given by the government. It is a right that the government can give to you and the government can take it away. The government can take away all of your civil rights and pronounce you to be a slave. The government does not have a right to make such a pronouncement because it conflicts with your basic human rights, but the government does have the power.

The issue of human rights can overlap with that of the civil rights. For example, the civil unrest in America in the late 1950's and 60's is called the Civil Rights struggle because it tended to focus on the legal rights of black Americans, but the struggle was so deep, so penetrating to all Americans, that the Civil Rights struggle was really a struggle for human dignity, for human rights. When the civil right involved is based on equality or liberty, then it begins to transcend the issue of the law and affects the dignity that all humans have from God.

When the government confuses the two, civil and human rights, the result is unhappy, and, invariably it is the human rights that suffer. When the government passes a law that favors one race over another, or one religion or ethnicity over another, it is disregarding the human rights of all of its citizens. It may enact such a law for whatever motive it finds suitable, but that does not change the simple fact, and it is a fact if you accept human rights, that the law is an abomination. Laws that enforced slavery were an abomination. A law that tends to degrade people based on race, sex, or their religion is an abomination. No less an abomination is a law that promotes one race, sex, or religion because it degrades each of us.

The federal complex has adopted laws that promote interests based on race and sex. The function of such laws is not to unite people as Americans, but to separate out different groups and emphasize to them that they are unable to function at the same level as other Americans and must have the protection of the federal government complex. These laws have been wonderful tools to accomplish the goal of splitting Americans. Moreover, there are many state and local officials who are in sympathy with the splitting of Americans and exacerbate the affect of these laws.

In truth, the federal complex is neutral regarding human and civil rights. It really does not care about them except in so far as they may be useful in the long term movement towards more control. The complex talks about civil rights and human rights to create dependence by certain groups, but basically the rights have no value to the complex one way or the other except as a tool to enhance its control. It thrives on raising money and establishing new legislation to counter anything it can whip up as a threat to human and civil rights while at the same time it undercuts the very basis of liberty and freedom. The complex wants to focus on "hate crimes" legislation as though murder is worse if the murderer thinks bad thoughts, but has no qualms about gutting the free market and the liberties Americans enjoy.

"For quartering large Bodies of armed Troops among us;

For protecting them, by mock Trial, from Punishment for any Murders which they should commit on the Inhabitants of these States;"

The Declaration of Independence, 1776

CHAPTER TEN

Professional and Private Armies

The charge in the indictment most dangerous to liberty is the federal complex's creation and maintenance of private armies. Does any person truly believe that private armies fostered by our own national government are consistent with personal liberty? They are now being used in foreign conflicts such as Afghanistan and Iraq where they develop their techniques for security and surveillance, and consume tens of billions of dollars in tax money.

Eventually the federal government complex will use them as muscle against its own citizenry. It may not do it this year or even this decade, but there will come a time when they will be used. It will do so because it can. They are too convenient a resource for the federal complex not to use them. The government can have illegal surveillance performed that can later be plausibly denied. These corporate armies come to the complex ready trained and will follow any instructions. Their employees are essentially amoral and will perform as they are instructed for money. While "amoral" sounds like a sweeping generalization, they do in fact perform as ordered for the money. They could not stay in business if they did not. And that business is security and surveillance. They do not have the qualms about operating against civilians that a drafted army or a part-time soldier, or even a community police force would have.

Do not be so naïve as to think that a democratic government cannot be persuaded to use private armies against their own citizens. It has already happened here. Hired armies have attacked Americans before, and at the orders of their own government. The first time was the Hessians, German mercenaries employed by George III. Hiring Hessians eased the King's recruitment problems. The private armies do the same thing for the federal complex. The complex is creating, sponsoring, and paying for private armies that eventually will be used against American citizens in our homes and our communities. It is a question of when.

Even aside from the threat to our liberty, private armies permit the federal complex to carry on aggressive conflicts that the American citizenry would not allow otherwise. These armies enable us to maintain wars where it would be unlikely that there would be sufficient military personnel available from our own armed services. Witness the differences between both Iraq and Afghanistan when compared to the experience with Vietnam. We have been able to pursue war in Afghanistan and Iraq with our existing military capabilities because the federal government has hired private armies to carry out some of the functions of the military. Without their active participation the chances of our success, whatever success is and however one measures it, in either country would be far slimmer. So Americans never have had to debate our role in Afghanistan or Iraq. Not like Vietnam was debated: civilians were drafted by the hundreds of thousands; fifty thousand young Americans were killed; the nation rumbled on the verge of civil insurrection; Johnson's presidency collapsed; and Nixon fled the capitol in disgrace, if not shame. Now, that was a debate!

The difference between Vietnam and both Iraq and Afghanistan is the draft. The drafting of young men is never popular. Each young person eligible for the draft seriously considers the wisdom of the federal government. The parents of this young person must weigh the fact that this child whom they have raised with love and devotion may come home in a body bag or be horribly damaged. Then there are the friends and relatives of this young person. When confronted with this physical taking of the person, and that is what a draft is, they must consider the war, its value, and its cost. This agonizing is barely less if the person is eligible for the draft, but remains home and untaken. The war puts that person's life on hold. It is difficult to make any plans longer than the date of the next draft round.

And the draft itself forces us to confront sticky issues. Who is getting drafted? Do young people in college get drafted? What if they are married? Are we going to draft women? Are some people somehow buying out of the draft? It is healthy for America to have to ask itself these questions. We confront questions not just of the war, but of class, and the nature of what it means to be an American.

War and occupation of other lands should not be taken lightly. War, by its nature, tears apart the country where it is being fought by Americans. We see horrendous pictures of it on television and other media, but the reaction is different when it is our sons and brothers who may be drafted to fight it next month. That damn war had better be worth it.

The professional and private armies distance the citizens from the wars. We can consider the issues with objectivity; there is less immediacy. Never mind the havoc and misery we create in the target country. We can settle back on our recliners with a calculator and keep a running tab of both the dollars and loss of life, and compare them with dollar benefits of improved trade, better access to raw materials such as oil, and general peace in the region. These are not calculations that a free people should use to inflict its might on another people. This is the shameful calculus of suffering, death, and impoverishment.

It is the professional and private armies that make those calculations possible. They give us distance. They allow us the luxury to consider more immediate issues, such as making our mortgage payment next month, and whether the Georgia Dawgs will finally beat the Florida Gators this year.

An unpopular military draft is a sign of a viable and vibrant democracy. A large professional army, any larger than is necessary to maintain readiness for immediate defense of a foreign threat and to train the draftees, is a sign of a secretive and potentially repressive regime. But to maintain both professional and private corporate armies is a disaster that is marking time.

It is the private armies who will seize dissidents, who will knock on your doors in the middle of the night with fraudulent warrants, who will operate the camps, and who will whisper to your employer that you are an undesirable. No matter whom you vote for in the next election, there will continue to be the private and professional armies. There is not one thing any American can do in the next election that will have any affect on this. That is because the problem is in the structure, the very fabric of the federal government complex.

States, individually and severally, must resist the complex. They should not allow the recruitment, training, or operations of private armies within their borders. These private armies should not be permitted to have police powers or engage in any type of surveillance or operation within these states. These states can make it clear to the federal complex that their citizens will not pay for the use or operation of these armies anywhere.

CHAPTER ELEVEN

Borders

The least subtle point to be made in this entire work is that it is generally acknowledged that a government has not merely the right but, indeed, the obligation to defend its citizens and its borders. It is difficult even to consider a plot of land to be a nation when its government is unable to defend its borders, but one whose government refuses to do so is virtually beyond imagination. It is impossible for a government to defend its citizens or its own integrity if it will not defend its borders. Yet this is what has happened in the United States.

The federal government complex has determined that it is in the best interests of the complex to maintain porous and essentially meaningless borders in the southeastern United States. The intent of the government complex is to encourage immigrants to enter these border states illegally. The complex does this in an effort to build up and fortify identifiable splinter groups which seek the protection of the complex and will contribute to and support the growth of the federal complex.

Not only has the government complex encouraged this immigration through the porous borders, but also through its offers of an extensive education, healthcare, and moral support system at no cost to the illegal immigrant. While these are attractive incentives, the federal complex has one more plum to offer: it encourages the illegal immigrants to maintain their language, customs and identity, to be and remain a splinter group dependent on the federal complex for protection and welfare. So the complex acts like the shepherd who not only allows the sheep to be stolen, but then also actively assists in the butchering and preparation of the pilfered lamb. Actually, it is worse than that. It is more like the shepherd who also insists that the remaining sheep assist the pilferage by paying the cost of the meat-cutting and the firewood. And then we come to the part that is a true outrage. If the sheep seek to protect themselves, then the shepherd rises in righteous anger and prohibits the sheep from taking any action. Where amnesty for the illegal immigrant fits into this already strained metaphor is for the reader to imagine.

The federal government complex has stated as clearly as possible that it intends to encourage further illegal immigration, and that the individual states will not be allowed to take any initiative to discourage that immigration or to protect their citizens. This has been the policy of the government complex for decades. It refuses to maintain the integrity of its borders and it expands incentives for illegals to enter. The government complex has a vested interest in the illegal immigration continuing. Occasionally when the citizenry becomes irate, the complex touts that it will put up a fence or hire more border guards. Then it awards amnesty for the illegals. For decades this policy of the government complex largely affected only the border states, but the immigrants have dispersed now to every state in the union. Still the main impact remains along the border states which have witnessed entire areas become worthless because of the trafficking in guns, drugs, and human beings.

The federal government, the complex, insists that the borders remain porous regardless of the government's duties and obligations to the nation. There is not one vote that will be cast in the next election that will change anything about illegal immigration in any substantive manner. There is not one vote that will be taken in Washington in any session from which the citizens in the border states can expect relief.

Because of the federal complex's abrogation of its responsibilities, the individual state governments have the obligation now to protect their citizenry. The border states as well as other states that are concerned about this issue should meet and establish a unified position. They must clearly set forth their grievance to the federal complex and indicate the steps that they, the states, intend to take. These steps should include at a minimum the defense of the state's own borders from foreign intrusion. Furthermore, the notice to the federal complex should affirm the state's determination to maintain this defense through the use of its militia forces.

The issue inescapably arises of paying for the defense of borders. When the federal government complex has abrogated its responsibility and done so on an issue that the federal government not only should pay for but has collected money from the state's citizens to do so, then the state should consider whether it has the obligation instruct its citizens to withhold that portion of money from the federal government to offset the state's own expenses. For the citizens of a state to continue to pay the federal complex to defend them when the announced policy of that complex is to refuse to do so, then any money collected for that purpose is no more than financial tribute similar to extortion.

The states driven to this desperate measure should not expect the complex to come to its senses. The complex is vested in illegal immigration. The citizenry in the various states must arouse the concern of their state governments to this issue and insist that their state governments protect them. The response of the federal complex, the Washington Establishment, will be that it is the will of the American people as expressed by the votes of their representatives that the borders remain porous. This is sheer nonsense. It is no more than the complex at work and an example of the affect of engineered splinter groups.

This is not a matter of states' rights or sovereignty. It is matter of state action to protect the citizenry and to force the federal complex to perform one of the few responsibilities for which the federal government was even called into existence by the states: to provide for the common defense.

"He has erected a Multitude of new Offices, and sent hither Swarms of Officers to harrass our People, and eat out their Substance,"

The Declaration of Independence, 1776

CHAPTER TWELVE

Growing the Federal Complex

This federal complex wants to succeed, it wants to grow and control American life. This section will raise just two major legislative initiatives that have provided the complex with moments of extraordinary growth.

The Income Tax

The bones of the federal complex were given extraordinary muscles in 1913 with the passing of the Sixteenth Amendment.

The federal government was then able to tax the income of its citizenry directly. It did not need to rely on the uncertain revenues of import duties and indirect taxes on the people. Nor did it any longer need assistance from the states. Instead of being financially dependent, the federal government became the source of money and power with the states scrambling to acquire some of the money that was given to the federal government by their own citizens. This ability to directly tax the citizenry has allowed the power of the federal government and complex to grow in an unbridled and bald-faced manner. The states, who were the source of the power of the federal government and to whom all powers not expressly granted the federal government were reserved, have become the poor relatives, fit only to monitor their insurance industries, marry and bury their citizens, and generally to scramble for federal money for their roads and schools.

The problem can be illustrated if we could assume that the citizens of each of the fifty states give the federal government one dollar for its revenue. The federal government then has a total of fifty dollars to spend. It requires dollars to operate but the rest is available and will be spent in various states for defense bases, education initiatives, public assistance, and so on. The states then begin to scramble to get whatever money they can from the federal government. It does not matter whether it is a good program, a bad program, nor does not it matter whether the state even wants the program. The point is that money is available and if Arkansas does not get it, New Jersey will. If Florida does not push for it, Montana will. Each state wants to get as much of the money as it possibly can. The winner is the state whose citizens give the federal government one dollar, but gets back a nickel more than their neighbor.

The election issue then becomes whether Senator So-and-So "brought home the bacon". If he did not, then he is in trouble; if he did, then he is accused of rolling the pork barrel and feeding in the trough. But all of this obscures the basic question of whether the federal complex should be dictating to every locale and state not only the programs, but the amount of money that it will receive back from what its citizens have sent the federal government. The issue is not that the government has gotten too big and we would all be happier if it would leave us alone. We have always known that. The federal government complex uses this money and these programs to undermine the Promise and Hope of America. They leave us gabbing about how well the legislators are doing emptying out the federal cornucopia while the basic issue, the extension of the complex's power is obfuscated. Citizens might say that this time they will only vote for the candidates who want smaller government and are fiscally conservative. The candidates then all say they want smaller government and are fiscally conservative. It makes no difference. The structure of the federal complex will determine the course, and that course is a steady wind that blows us towards control by the complex and loss of liberty. Instead of voting for the federal candidate who makes the best promises, vote for the one with the biggest shoe size, or the pointiest head, or the best legs. It will achieve the same result and you will have a lot more fun.

These officials, this government complex, seek to expand the government and re-design the electorate. So far they have succeeded admirably. You can know that it has succeeded because it does not matter for whom you vote in the next election, it will have no substantive impact on the direction in which the wind is blowing. End the federal income tax. Let the federal complex come to Atlanta, Albany, Salt Lake City, and forty-seven other state capitals for its financing.

Healthcare

Healthcare in America is an amazing amalgam of health resources and organizations some of which are government owned, some privately owned, and everything in between. Virtually all healthcare in America is at least as good as what is available anywhere else in the world and overall is probably superior. It is unusual for Americans in any number to seek healthcare in foreign countries.

The problem with American healthcare is that it is so expensive. The dollars spent as a percent of our GDP is extraordinary and the most remarkable thing is the steady rate of climb. The federal and state governments pay for the bulk of healthcare through Medicare and Medicaid with a number of other special programs. The largest percentage of it is spent by Medicare on those persons who are over sixty-five or are eligible for other programs. Medicare began in the 1960's with President Johnson. At the time Medicare was set up to pay the hospitals and other institutional providers on the basis of their cost, not on their charges. Congress did not want to pay the going rate. It figured that the best way to pay the providers was to pay them what it cost to offer the care to the Medicare patients. After all, the government figured it was entitled to that discount from charges because many of the people who were being covered by Medicare otherwise would not have been able to pay for their care, so the provider was getting something. Additionally the thought that some institution or person would make a profit from Medicare was unpalatable.

So, Medicare gave itself a discount by paying cost. It seemed like a good idea at the time. Let us take an over-simplified example: a hospital is going to be paid by Medicare and needs to figure out how much Medicare will pay to the hospital for its services. The hospital can figure how much it cost to take care of each patient or its cost per patient-day by taking its total costs for a year and dividing by the number of patients or patient-days in the year. With more sophisticated accounting the hospital can also figure out how much it cost to care for persons with specific diagnoses by seeing how long the person was in the hospital and the services those particular patients use.

Medicare, though, does not want to pick up every cost because it says its patients do not use every service. An example is the cost the hospital sustains to operate its neonatal intensive care unit. Medicare figures that its patients do not use obstetrical services, so why should any cost associated with that unit be included in the cost it pays. So there are costs that a hospital has that Medicare will not include in its calculations. But the hospital still has these costs; somebody has got to pay for them. Otherwise the hospital cannot offer them. So, these costs get passed along to the patient who pays out-of-pocket or pays with a commercial insurance. Those patients pay more than they would pay otherwise because the government takes a discount.

In practice Medicare's calculations have become very sophisticated and there is an extraordinary bureaucracy that carries out the congressional mandates for care and for reimbursement to institutions. The Medicare calculations change constantly as it makes adjustments to pay for hospitals, doctors, home health, and so on. But the point that is important here is that Medicare uses that same cost-based payment philosophy for institutional providers that it used in the 1960's. In fact, the correct terminology is not that Medicare is "paying" providers; instead, Medicare is "reimbursing" them.

So, what has been the result of this philosophy? The result has been healthcare costs that have sailed through the roof and give every indication of continuing their upward climb. Something is wrong with this model. We know that not only from the fact that healthcare keeps eating up larger chunks of out GDP, but because of other anomalies in healthcare. For example, healthcare is the only industry in America where technological advances have dramatically increased costs to the consumer, not cut them. How can this be? How can healthcare eat so much of our economy? Why is there no relief in sight?

The answer is right in front of us. Let us return for a moment to the 1960's when Medicare was being considered. Lyndon Johnson was president; the country still mourned the loss of Kennedy; and Vietnam was gathering steam but had not yet erupted. America was one of two great superpowers, the other being the Soviet Union. America and the Soviet Union appeared locked in a nuclear deathgrip from which it was feared that neither might emerge. The Soviet Union in reality was a powerful military machine, but its economy was really worse than pre-war America's. A quarter century later, it would collapse. But no one knew that then.

By comparison, America was immensely rich. Its post-war economy was growing by leaps and bounds. Never in the history of the world had so many lived so well. Despite the looming menace of the Soviet Union, the early sixties was a time of unbridled optimism socially, morally, and economically, and justifiably so. Americans could afford that optimism because of the great economy, and the reason for this great economy was simple: it was based on a free market/competitive model. The federal complex was witnessing the greatest and most powerful wealth producing engine the world had ever seen. It was a proven winner. And what did the complex do?

Instead of using the winner, the competitive free market model, the government said "I know best. I want a cost-based system." Basically, it told the institutional providers that it would pay costs, whatever those costs worked out to be. The rest, as they say, is history. Costs have gone where no man has gone before. Instead of riding the most powerful economic horse in history, the government fell back on the old nag of cost-based reimbursement. It is still riding that nag and wondering what went wrong.

Periodically one politician or another in Washington screams bloody murder that healthcare costs are out of control, and killing our economy. In fact there is a chorus singing that tune every time that there is a serious effort at balancing the budget. What they do not harmonize on is the simple fact that the healthcare system now is doing exactly what any other industry would do with the same incentives and exactly what Congress designed the system to do: drive the costs through the roof. Furthermore, the federal complex has deliberately sought to stifle any competition by eliminating as many institutional competitors as possible in any given market. The result is that the costs sail more quickly to the stratosphere.

Even aside from the healthcare cost issue is the immense cost of administering this cost-based system. The administration of this system is itself an industry with a bureaucracy replete with thousands of experts, consultants, and lobbyists. They are not evil or bad. Administration of the cost-based system is an industry now like any other. They want to tweak and twist the system. This system provides the government complex with control over the operations of institutional healthcare providers. Instead of a relative handful of federal employees stoking a competitive model, there is a vast bureaucracy monitoring institutional costs. In affect it provides the federal complex with control over the healthcare industry without having to actually seize the assets. It begins to look more like a socialist system without the federal complex having to go through the political turmoil of seizing the system outright. The controls grow steadily and thoroughly each year. For the complex the whipped cream topping is that after decades of cost-based reimbursement which has resulted in decades of unbridled cost increases, the federal complex can claim that the present system is too expensive and this country has to have socialized healthcare to save it. One must admit that there is a certain beauty to the symmetry of the federal complex developing policies that create the cost problems in the industry, then seizing the industry in an effort to hold the costs down. Actually, we see this pattern again and again: the complex creates the chaos and then claims it must destroy the system to save us.

The last thing the complex wants to consider is allowing the free market to make the system rational. The free market grabs industries by the scruff of their neck, shoves them down, and holds them there until they scream "uncle". The free market is the ninja of economic systems. It shows no mercy. If it did we would all still be riding in buggies and complaining about the smell of horse poop in the streets.

Unfortunately, the free market acts only in a peripheral way in healthcare and in areas where there is minimal government reimbursement. The federal complex will not now change to a different and more rational model. It will not give full rein to the market forces. It will not voluntarily give up the vested interest it has in cost-based reimbursement; nor will it ever unleash the power of the common man and a competitive marketplace. It does not matter whom you vote for in the next election, it will not change. It cannot change.

Unless states take action, the only real issue is when, not if, the government will control the entire healthcare system. It will happen, and, ironically it will happen under the guise of getting control of the upward spiraling costs which the government has created.

Faith and Hell

Many years ago a great man said that faith is the evidence of things unseen. Americans have never lacked faith: faith in the Creator, faith in themselves, and faith in the goodness of their intentions. When we see our own boat, this ship of state, blown ever closer to danger, we must have faith that we can bring the boat about and take it to a safer harbor. It was done in the 1770's and it can be done now.

America is the greatest nation that has ever seen the sun. Its greatness is not to be found in its natural blessings and beauty, though they are plentiful, nor is it found in its government, which two hundred years ago was a godsend. Instead its greatness is found in the people, in the common man, and his belief in himself and his own strength and determination. I have not the slightest doubt that if a million common Americans were transported to the deepest jungle, or to a barren desert, in a few years these men and women would again build a great nation. This is not an empty boast. One nation whose nature is close to our own, Israel, did this very thing barely fifty years ago. Give the common man a Promise and a Hope, and there is nothing he cannot do.

It was this American, the common man, who built the nation. He's still here, three hundred million strong. But he is on that damn sailboat and the boat is getting blown towards the rocks. He can stop it. He can do it by insisting that the creators of the federal government, the individual states, move the boat away from the rocks. That is the hope.

America has always dared to reinvent itself. In the 1770's we were three million people clinging precariously to the Atlantic seaboard. A hundred years later we were growing into an industrial powerhouse that spanned the continent. And a hundred years after that America was one of two great superpowers in the world and shortly to be the only one. Americans are always willing to confront the future because the future is the substance of our faith.

Our faith in a decent and generous future makes us different from other nations, different from other people. There are people who choose of their own free will to live in hell. People who choose to live in hell do not smile on those who do not. They want to kill them for not having chosen the same. There are also people who choose to be slaves rather than free. People who choose to be slaves do not wish well to those who do not make the same choice. They seek to kill them for choosing liberty. There are always people who will trade their liberty for security. They will not be grateful to those who do not; they will curse them and pray for them to starve.

This is not easy for Americans to accept. Americans always want to believe the best in other people. We want to believe that if people are given the choice between freedom and slavery, they will always choose freedom. We believe it because for the past five hundred years we have born witness on this continent to the power of the common man, to the miracle of the Promise and the Hope of America.

It is difficult for Americans to consider that there are people who prefer to live in ignorance, slavery, and poverty because their fathers so lived or because they have a religion or way of life that demands it. But history instructs us that this is so, and the instruction has come in the form of that terrible and bloody teaching method that history uses. How many wars or actions has America fought in which the people we thought we were liberating have been left worse off or at least no better off than they were before the war despite the deaths of so many young Americans, simply because the people of that country did not value or want liberty?

There are those among us who do not value their liberty. Know that there are many states that will not come forward to protect the liberty of their citizens from the depredations of the federal complex. The next chapter explores possible paths for those states that will do so. There are states that will not surrender, that will do whatever is in their power to protect their citizens. These few, these courageous states must be supported.

"But when a long Train of Abuses and Usurpations, pursuing invariably the same Object, evinces a Design to reduce them under absolute Despotism, it is their Right, it is their Duty, to throw off such Government, and to provide new Guards for their future Security."

The Declaration of Independence, 1776

CHAPTER THIRTEEN

The Action Plan

If you have managed to wade through this far, I would encourage you to put the book down and consider whether you agree with the general premises that have been set forth. Certainly none of the general information or statistics you have encountered is particularly revolutionary or eye-opening. You have seen it before in one form or another. No, it is the

174

premises put forward that you should mull over before proceeding further. Do you agree that there is a federal complex that pushes the governance of America as surely as a sailboat is moved in a stiff and steady wind? Do you agree that this complex is largely impervious to election-day results? Do you agree that in the end the complex and the splinter groups will kill the Promise and the Hope of America for the common man? That it is killing them now and our liberty with them?

Find a shady spot on a bright afternoon, put your feet up, and cogitate upon those few questions. Do not lightly answer them in the affirmative unless you are certain. It is far easier to deny them, close the book, and drift off into a pleasant nap. Once you say "Yes", and admit that the underlying assumptions may be correct, you will not vote, or support candidates, or watch the political process from the same perspective as before. That, my friend, is because you know which way the wind blows.

And the problem with knowing this is that you may look inside yourself and find that you have the courage to do something about it. So often the reason we are hesitant to act is not that we fear that we will not see the courage in ourselves to bring about change, but that we will find that we do have the courage. And where does finding the courage leave us? It leaves us in 1776, that's where. So, put the book down now while there is still time, go have a drink, and write a note on your social blog that you are damn well fed up and are going to send ten dollars to the Democrats or Republicans. Or send five to each, because it really makes no difference and that way you can make twice as many people happy.

What, you're still here? I will assume then you accept the general premise that the federal complex will continue growing its control of the federal government until we have a managed economy and a complete loss of liberty. This is evident from the splintering of the citizenry into groups who feel that they must rely on the government for protection.

I assume that you generally concur with the premise that federal officials whom you elect cannot or will not make any substantive difference for the reasons discussed earlier and any others you may care to add. There is tremendous pressure from inside of the federal complex for the complex to expand its control over American life, and the complex enjoys the growing support from the splinter groups. The goal of the complex is to increase its control. The Promise and Hope of America are simply unintended casualties, "collateral damage".

Still reading? Then the burden has attached. You are transported back to 1776 and are confronted with prickly options. These are issues of liberty and human rights, and courage and reason.

The states must act to restore this balance. Seek to put people into office in your state capitols who will act to preserve your liberty from the federal complex. It must be the states.

There are simply no other entities in America that can do it. The states were the ones who invented America, who invented the Promise and the Hope, who entered the fray for liberty. It was the states, thirteen of them, that turned loose the common man. These states, now fifty in all, have that same duty to maintain and ensure the liberty of their citizens. Yes, even when liberty is threatened by the states' own creation, this federal government and complex.

Instead of wasting time and money on the federal legislature, focus on your state representatives. This should be a more direct and easier process than approaching or affecting the federal candidates. This is not a time for questions such as whether they are willing to balance the state's own budget. That time has long since passed. It is a time to ask the candidate whether they will protect the citizenry from the overreaching of the federal government. Can they say that they are willing "to pledge our Lives, our Fortunes, and our sacred Honor" in defense of freedom? Are there men and women who will call the federal complex to account in their state legislatures?

The federal government did not will itself into power. It never even sought approval to exist directly from the people, the citizenry. The federal government was a creature of the states from the beginning. The only reason for its existence was to bring some uniformity among the relations of the states and to address common issues in a common manner.

The Founders expected that the federal government would tend to restrict liberty, that its sheer size and momentum would lead it to interfere with the rights of the individual. So in addition to the internal balances of power, and the external balance of the states, the Founders enacted the Bill of Rights. This Bill of Rights is not a grant of rights to the citizenry. The Founders believed that the rights were given us by God. It is not the province of the government to either grant or restrict them. In fact, it would be hubris for the government to presume to grant them, and an insult to both God and man to restrict them. The foundation of these rights is set forth in the Declaration of Independence: we are born human. What could be simpler in theory or more difficult in practice? Instead the Bill of Rights is addressed to the federal government. They are a set of instructions to the federal government which prohibit it from interfering in certain areas of people's lives or the powers of the states. It should better be called the Bill of Nots.

But even within the Bill of Rights, this protection of liberty through prohibitions, is embedded still another layer of protection. It is the final protection that the Founders could give us: the Second Amendment. With the Second Amendment the founders recognized that the true saviors of liberty are ourselves. We are the final balance to the power of the federal government. The federal government is prohibited from interfering with the citizenry as we obtain the arms to defend our liberty from an oppressive government. The Founders expected that the citizenry would arm, form militias, and put those militias into motion if need arose. The Founders had just done that same thing.

The Second Amendment is not about deer hunting, or protecting ourselves from invasions from Spain, or Canada, or England. The Founders were acknowledging the right of the citizenry to defend liberty from an oppressive national government: to arm, and defend the gifts received from God. Our liberty is not a bonus from the federal government, or the Constitution, or the Declaration of Independence. Liberty is a God-given gift which a government can honor to its blessing or ignore at its peril. The Founders expected the States to form militias as a counterbalance.

The purpose of this book is not to foment rebellion or secession. It is most definitely not to encourage violence or threats of violence. The very term "secession" suggests a complete break with the federal government, and conjures up horrors from our not so distant past. Instead it is to urge the creation of a counterbalance to the power of the complex. Creating this counterbalance may require disunion, that is, changing the manner in which some states relate to the federal government. This proposed disunion invites sanity, not violence. It establishes a counterbalance to the federal complex. It restores the liberty envisioned and defended in the 1770's.

It might unfold thusly: states that are willing to step forward to protect their citizens first pass a simple resolution in their legislature condemning the unwarranted control of the federal complex in the lives of their citizenry. They then pass a resolution authorizing an individual or individuals to meet with the representatives of other states to discuss specific grievances and propose an appropriate coordinated response. Meanwhile the congressional representatives of each such state should make his or her state's resolution known in their respective chamber, the Senate or the House, and request that no further business be conducted by that body until the resolution can be addressed. Furthermore, the member should request that representatives be appointed from the federal complex to meet with the representatives of the states which have passed the resolution to discuss an outcome.

I would anticipate that at least on the surface the federal complex will ignore these voices at the state level, pretend that it does not hear, and proceed with business as usual all the while hoping that the voices go away. When the resolutions are read in Congress, then the federal complex will turn and snarl malevolently.

For the reasons discussed earlier, there will not be more than a handful of states which pass such a resolution and empower representatives to meet together. However, that will be enough to move forward and carry the central demand: that the citizenry of these states are no longer willing to remain in communion with a federal complex whose actions evidence ruination and the end of liberty.

Let us believe that at this point the federal complex comes to its senses, realizes the error of its ways and restores liberty through a series of Constitutional amendments that create a counterbalance to the federal complex by empowering the states. That is the way it should be. Just like King George did. Right? Get real. There is too much power, too much money at stake. Because it is unclear as to what might happen, let us follow a white rabbit.

Recent Fantastical Developments in a Parallel Universe

We tumble down a rabbit hole to enter a parallel universe where things are rarely as they seem though in this similar universe there is a nation much like ours on a planet much like ours with a history much like ours, but of course being fantasy and make-believe, it is not ours. In this alternative nation let us imagine that eight states have passed a resolution condemning their federal government complex, and that the congressional representatives of these states have made their resolutions known in their respective chambers. In this parallel universe no one in the federal complex has a shoe size larger than three so they can easily be recognized. Their little feet force them all to walk with tiny mincing steps that are a source of great merriment among the press corps.

The federal complex held its breath when the resolutions were read in their congress, but moved on with business. Meanwhile representatives of the several states met in committee, a committee that in this parallel universe was called the Several States Committee, and passed a resolution urging that the several states should each pass a resolution obligating each state to pay directly into the federal coffers an amount equal to the amount that their own citizens otherwise would pay directly to the federal treasury in income taxes. The citizens of these states were to be directed to pay their income taxes to the treasury of their respective state, not the federal treasury. This would ensure that the complex was fully funded, but that these particular states did not want the complex to tax its citizens directly. It was a withdrawal by these states from the effects of the Sixteenth Amendment. Because this was a resolution of the Several States Committee and did not have the force of law in any particular state, this still did not provoke a general response from the federal complex other than more nasty snarls and veiled threats. The complex began to portray the Several States Committee members as racist hate-mongers and neo-Nazis. The complex contemplated legal action against the Several States Committee and several members went into hiding.

Two of the eight states put the matter directly to their own citizens in the form of referendums while six others considered the matter in their legislatures. In the end four of the several states passed laws instructing their citizens that commencing in ninety days, they were to send tax money owed on their income not to Washington, but to the state's own income tax commissions in the state capitols. This action by the four states precipitated the crisis. The members of the federal complex set up a howl. Some demanded immediate military action against the states and stomped their tiny feet. While there was a great deal of sympathy among the various splinter groups for this type of action, cooler heads prevailed. There had been no suggestion on the part of any of the states or any statements by the Several States Commission of anyone actually leaving the union. In fact, it was clear in all the statements that the leaving option, "secession" in the common tongue, was not on the table. At least not in the way that secession had been historically understood. The word alone called up images of cannons, and blue and gray armies on the move even in this parallel universe. So the word was avoided or at least used in a different manner. There, "secession", when used at all, was meant to suggest that the states were considering relating to the federal government in a different manner, a non-traditional manner, as yet unspecified.

But make no mistake, there was a sundering and a great nation began to transform.

At this point the story diverged into two lines. In one the federal complex and the Several States Committee, both anxious to avoid any action that drove the other beyond a peaceful resolution, met and agreed to revise the manner in which the several states related to the federal complex which itself was receiving greater scrutiny even from its supporters. In the second and grimmer scenario the federal complex did nothing until the states actually began to gather money. Then the federal complex moved through a series of federal indictments to arrest groups of state legislators and the members of the Several States Committee for conspiring to violate federal laws. This involved unleashing federal marshals and various other federal enforcement agencies as well as members of the private armies who already had been employed extensively in surveillance. In the councils of the federal complex, this appeared to be the right move. They would appear strong and swift, and their response moderate and targeted.

However, in fact the scenario did not play as expected. In two of the states the legislators were seized in their chambers in the state capitols by federal officials without violent incident, but in two other states, armed guards refused to permit the federal officials to advance and make arrests. This resulted in stand-offs. Then armed citizens and militias began to arrive at the sites of the stand-offs. In one state capitol the federal officials backed away and left. In the other state one side or the other opened fire in the stand-offs and there were several deaths on both sides. Although the battle casualties were lop-sided against the state militias and the citizens, the legend of their resistance took hold and the casualties became martyrs and heroes, the last thing the complex wanted.

The two states where the legislators had been arrested without violent incident then stiffened and began taking federal law enforcement agents as prisoners. Several cities did so on their own initiative, calling it protective custody. A few other states, not members of the original Several States Committee, asked to send representatives to that committee. They were refused until their legislative bodies passed a version of the original resolution. Three of those states did so which increased the total number of member in the Several States Committee to seven. Two states were now using the "s" word and were calling up detachments of their militia.

The uncertainty and confusion worsened when a few counties located in the several states declared that they were unwilling to follow any further dictates from their state capitols. This action was encouraged by the complex. The complex was heartened until numerous counties in states which were not members of the Committee passed resolutions threatening to secede from their states and send delegates to the Several States.

In several of these "rogue" counties armed groups of citizens began closing down stretches of interstate highways and menacing rail and air travel.

The federal complex looked hard at its options. Their initial response had done nothing more than provoke violence. At that point the complex had to begin some type of negotiations or expand and escalate the armed conflict. A number of considerations led them in the direction of negotiations. First was to give everyone time to cool down. Second was that federal officials recoiled at the thought of using military and para-military troops against their own citizens on their own soil. The third, and probably the pivotal factor, was that the complex itself was coming under serious pressure from commercial interests concerned with the possibility of a total and indefinite economic disruption. Additionally, the foundations, lobbyists, law firms, commissions, others who comprised the federal complex sensed that their roles might actually expand: they might make more money in a nation experiencing disunion and constitutional transformation.

Federal officials offered to consider calling a convention to consider possible modifications to the Constitution and the Bill of Rights. The new Several States Committee declined citing their concerns that their demands for liberty should not be subjected to votes substantially controlled by splinter groups and in which they had no confidence. They insisted that they would meet together first to determine their own course. By that time three other states had passed resolutions and also joined the Several States Committee. Let us leave at least the forward progress in this parallel universe and hope for their sakes that they had the sense to avoid violence, re-knit their union, and use their leverage only to develop a counterbalance to the power of the federal complex.

Still, it is worthwhile to look at some of the actions that this Several States Committee recommended, starting with the proposal that the states insist that the money sent to the federal coffers by their citizens pass first through the state government. For the states to enact this does not deny the federal government any of its tax revenue. All it would mean is that the states, not the Internal Revenue Service, would collect the tax money. To say "all it would mean", above, is somewhat glib, because in this parallel universe the federal government could not allow that to occur without a reaction. Not only did it violate numerous laws and the power granted the federal government by their constitution, but it was a direct challenge to the federal purse. Members of the Several States Committee surely knew that such a challenge would precipitate whatever action the federal government intended to take.

In effect these states told their federal complex that the cause of liberty trumped their constitution. It also trumped federal legislation, and umpteen thousand court decisions. The federal government could not both accept this and leave their constitution intact. The federal complex had to either bring the states to heel or accept that their constitution would have to be fundamentally restructured. It might have been easier if the several states had declared for secession; these states would have gone outside the pale and could be treated as hostiles. Here, the several states wanted to stay under the umbrella, but in a way that protected the liberty of their citizens from the complex. That made it difficult for the federal complex to justify a military seizure of the states. Furthermore, such an action could have driven states to take an irrevocable stand to secede.

Between the time that the Several States Committee made its recommendations and the time that four states acted on them, members of the federal complex would have personally sought out their acquaintances and counterparts in the state capitols in an effort to forestall any formal action. Heavens knows what threats were made or rewards promised for stopping any state action. There must have been similar pressure brought to bear on members of the state legislatures. Certainly as the time for the votes in the state capitols drew closer, the federal complex would push strongly.

Every state did not join the Several States Committee. This was due to the success of the splintering of the electorate by the complex, and because there were always those who would trade liberty for federal largesse. Furthermore, many people may have imagined that they could fix everything in the next election, or even that the loss of liberty was not a bad thing. Perhaps some would feel more comfortable in an autocratic state where decisions would not weigh on them; it could not come too soon. For whatever reason, the citizens of every state in the parallel universe simply did not want to act to restore the balance. Even in some of those states where the citizenry did want to restore the balance, many were too fearful of acting to do so.

Recall that our own rebellion from England was developed by a minority of the citizenry. Had there been a general referendum almost certainly the vote to separate ourselves from England would not have passed. One might even draw a parallel with the issue in Russia between the Bolsheviks and the Mensheviks. Confronting the federal complex will require bold and courageous leadership. It will require men and women who are determined to face threats, hardships, and the full weight of reprisals by the federal complex.

In this parallel universe, these states were telling the federal government that although a law had been passed by their congress and had been signed into law by their president, that their citizens would not be forced to forgo liberty or pay for something to which they strenuously objected. This was telling their federal complex that their constitution as it had been traditionally understood and as it had been interpreted by the courts, did not work any longer in all situations. It was also telling the complex that a majority vote within the Congress should not always be determinative or binding on the nation.

This is scary in any universe, but even if you disagree with everything that has been put down here, consider the question whether a majority vote in the government complex should always override the objections of the minority. And consider whether it makes a difference to your answer if the majority vote in the complex does not represent the actual desire of the majority of the people. Moreover, consider that the majority vote may be manufactured by the federal complex's successful use of splinter groups. Is this fair? Is this a democracy?

In this other universe the states insisted that the liberty and freedom of their citizens trumped the greed and power-mongering of the federal complex. This was not an issue of states' rights or of firing on Fort Sumter. It was an issue of states' obligations, the obligations that each state had to protect the liberty of its citizens.

This was also a re-thinking of their constitution. It was almost certainly a new constitutional convention called by some or all of the states. There was the distinct possibility that a new federal government could emerge, one in which the center of gravity had shifted back to the state houses and local arenas. The majority of states may have been delighted with the federal complex and wanted to keep it exactly as it was. A minority of states may have wanted to relate to the federal government in a different fashion, but within the federal umbrella. It is possible that not all states would be part of the new union in a manner identical to the others.

Liberty will be protected when the states stop wagging their tails for supper like fifty dogs at the master's door, scrambling for scraps and bones. Far better for the states to tell the federal government what their citizens will accept and pay for. There will be states that have structured themselves to depend on the largesse of the federal complex; they cannot and will not respond. These are states that will not balance their budgets without assistance from other states in the form of federal handouts. Other states will have allowed splinter groups to be manufactured and developed into identifiable blocs that may even control the statehouses; they cannot and will not respond.

Disunion and Beyond

America's constitution has been largely unchanged since the 1780's. It was a radical vision even though it embodied ideas, such as democracy, that were thousands of years old. The Founders, for all of their human flaws and faults, did a magnificent job. They created a government framework that nourished the common man.

Now the government practices that have grown out of this framework should change. There must be a counterbalance to the complex. The complex will not change willingly, will not give up power without the threat of disunion, and, perhaps not even then. Disunion is not secession. Secession suggests a complete break as was attempted in the 1860's. Disunion is not such a break. It is the opportunity for a state to declare that it will not allow the federal government to proceed along a ruinous path. It is not a matter of a majority vote because the principles at issue are the foundations of our freedom, of what was set forth as our most fundamental beliefs in the Declaration of Independence. If a majority seeks to enslave themselves or others, they are wrong. No person should consider himself or herself bound by such a vote. Nor is the legitimacy of such a vote enhanced by the active presence of the splinter groups.

There must be a counterbalance to the growing power of the federal complex. On issues central to our liberty, a state must have the freedom to decline to participate, to refuse to subject its citizens to further encroachment. It makes no difference whether a state has the right to do so. Whatever rights a state may or may not have been accorded by the Constitution or the courts are irrelevant. A state's greater obligation is to its citizens. This was so in 1776, and it is so now.

The development of viable political frameworks that promote the principles of the Declaration of Independence did not go into a freeze after the 1780's. There are other approaches, other frameworks, other constitutions that can better preserve our most basic principles, the beliefs that make us Americans. Do not sit back and pretend that these issues are better considered only by the pundits or the professional politicos. Neither the pundit nor the professional politician gave us either the Declaration of Independence or the Constitution two hundred years ago. They were not even consulted. There is no reason to consult them now. It is a job for the common man.

Can we really not think of a better system? Must we really have a circus every few years where our choices are old hacks or media darlings whose main qualifications are two rows of bright shining teeth and big money? Men and women whom we would not have as friends, with whom we would not break bread, we elect to high office to govern us. The Founders thought of a pretty good framework in the 1780's; cannot we do the same? Have we grown so stupid in the last two hundred years that we cannot think for ourselves? Of course not. There's a better way!

America's unique contribution to the moral and political world view is our Declaration of Independence and our Bill of Rights. The Declaration of Independence set forth the simple truth that every man and woman is born free. God never once made a slave- not a slave to a prince, a president, a chairman, a fuehrer, or to the Almighty Dollar. Not even to Himself. We are free not due to any efforts of the Republicans or the Democrats; but by virtue of the grace of God. Because we are born free we have a right to enjoy certain perquisites: life, liberty, and the pursuit of happiness. There are no "buts". Each person has the God-given right to live in a manner he or she chooses as well as he or she is able.

This simple ethic gave birth to the greatest nation on earth. There is a causal relationship between this freedom and our greatness. It is not an accident or a simple coincidence. The world is replete with far older nations and far older cultures. It is barely five hundred years since the settlement of this hemisphere by Europeans even began.

America is not an accident of geography and natural blessings. Europeans did not simply come to America, commit genocide, and take over the blessings. It is stupid to ask, "how could anyone miss?" Look around at the misses: Russia, Southeast Asia, or sub-Saharan Africa. Look at the oil producing countries today. The difference is not geography or natural blessings, though undeniably they have been plentiful in America. The difference is the American people. The difference is that we deny that God ever made a slave. Governments have made billions of them, but God not one. Who are you going to trust?

Our extraordinary success has not been an accident. It is a direct result of our acknowledgement and belief in the truth that people are born free: that every man and every woman is entitled to roll the bones on a flat table. This belief has unleashed the greatest of human powers, a force unstoppable in the course of human events: the uncommon power of the common man.

America loves its geniuses and its stars; we come near worshipping them. But geniuses and stars did not build America into the nation it is. They may have inspired it, they may have pointed new ways, or they may only have ridden our success. What has built America is the common man doing uncommon things and doing them day in and day out until they cease to be uncommon. America's success gushes up from the efforts of the common man. In the long run every nation may not get the governance that it thinks it should have, but it will get the one it deserves. We must have courage now.

Now quit wasting time with some old book. Have a party with your neighbors and figure out who your state representatives are. Then get after them. Get busy!

ABOUT THE AUTHOR

J. Peterson is the author's pen name. He has the great honor and privilege to be a practicing attorney. He believes that the Declaration of Independence is the greatest document penned in the last five hundred years. The author is most grateful for all of his blessings not least of which is that he and his family live in the most beautiful city in the world. He is deeply indebted to the heroic story of the American common man as the inspiration for this work.